Date Due

WOMEN OF TO-DAY

DAME LAURA KNIGHT.

WOMEN OF TO-DAY

by

MARGARET COLE

Illustrated

Essay Index Reprint Series

BOOKS FOR LIBRARIES PRESS, INC.

FREEPORT, NEW YORK

First Published 1938
Reprinted 1968

LIBRARY OF CONGRESS CATALOG CARD NUMBER:
68-16920

PRINTED IN THE UNITED STATES OF AMERICA

CONTENTS

ILLUSTRATIONS

ETHEL SMYTH

WOMEN OF TO-DAY

I

ETHEL SMYTH

ACCORDING to Ethel Smyth herself, the first thing in her life which she clearly remembers is leaping out of a low pony-carriage which was going up St. Mary Cray Hill near Sidcup and finding herself on her back in the road—because, being very young, she had not noticed that her elders, when jumping out, were careful to jump in the direction in which the carriage was proceeding. We have no date for this *contretemps*, nor is there any drawing or photograph of it available ; but it is easy enough to picture to oneself this small and sturdy child lying on her back in the mud, surrounded by the nest of petticoats which nicely-brought-up mid-Victorian children wore, waving in the air legs cased in white cotton stockings and black half-boots, and—if we may judge from her subsequent career—shrieking for help in a furious bawl.

For Ethel Smyth has always had a loud voice, both literally and metaphorically ; at the Crystal Palace in youth, when a surge of the crowd temporarily parted her from her parents, she cried, " I shall never see my Papa and Mamma again ! " in such an agonized roar that she was instantly reunited to them ; and she has never hesitated either to ask frequently and clearly for what she wanted (and small success would have been hers if she had), or to express her frank opinion about people and circumstances when she felt like it, even if it would have been more tactful to hold her tongue.

" I wish," somebody once said to some of her relatives, " that your sister could be persuaded to *pretend* to like Elgar's music, even if she doesn't. People are certain to put down this openly expressed dislike to jealousy."

It is not surprising that her friend Mrs. Benson, wife of an Archbishop of Canterbury, who found it difficult to understand the meaning of many of the technical terms which musical critics use, was delighted to meet the phrase " a loud allusion to a former subject in the bass " —for that so obviously referred to her friend Ethel's style of conversation.

Ethel Smyth is a composer, and though not an infant prodigy, has been a composer since her childhood. And her life illustrates so well the special difficulties which composers have to face, particularly composers who want to live in an unmusical country like England, and more particularly composers who are careless enough to be

4

born women, that it would be tempting, in this short study, to confine oneself to those aspects of it. But to do so would be to paint a very incomplete picture, and to leave out half of a splendidly robust and challenging personality.

Ethel Smyth is not only a composer ; she is a person of tremendous physical and mental energy, as is shown by her habit of bumping, dashing, and rushing about, her passion for tramping and games, and the vigour with which she can take up causes. In the full tide of her musical career she took up women's suffrage for some years with all the energy of which she was capable—of course on the side of the militants.

She has a passion for making friends, both of men and women ; and though her acquaintances have laughed at the enthusiasm which she shows in her friendships—one says that they begin with an " Oh, what a woman ! " period, which lasts for about two years, and that there-after the fervour gradually subsides until after about seven years the time is ripe for a new transport to begin— nevertheless she herself says that she has never grown out of or forgotten any friendships, even one which was sharply ended in full tide ; it is only that she is always capable of finding fresh excitement and delight in a new personality. Of course, a genius for friendship often carries with it also a gift for antipathy, and there have been people whom Ethel Smyth could not endure and who could not endure her. It is related that, at the

5

height of her friendship with the Mrs. Benson mentioned above, she had to be smuggled, as it were, into Lambeth Palace by a back entrance where the Archbishop could not see her, since the mere sight of that tempestuous personality was enough to upset the archiepiscopal calm for the day ! It is surely, however, some claim to fame to have been able to produce so violent an effect on a Prince of the Church.

Further, she is intensely sociable ; she loves dining out—but not dancing, at least in youth, because the men would dance out of time and her musical ear could not bear it. She likes horses and enormous and alarming dogs, and games and physical exercises of all sorts, the latter to an extent which scandalized her German musical friends, who could not believe that a musician in possession of her senses could weep real tears at the prospect of being unable to hunt. She was prouder, she says, when Sayers, the professional golfer, complimented an approach shot of hers than she was of any praise received for her music ; and on one occasion, having a chance to spend a few days with a friend whom she seldom saw, as he lived out of England, she insisted on his coming to stay at North Berwick in the winter (he not being a golfer), dragged him all the time round the links, and finished by hitting him on the head with a golf ball !

Finally, she has a lively sense of Society, with a capital S, and a vivid appreciation of the upper classes. She was a great friend of the Empress Eugénie, and has always enjoyed the Royal Family. In one of her books she quotes a scrap of conversation overheard about herself. " Ethel Smyth ? I like her music, but I've never met her. An awful snob, isn't she ? " " Oh, terrific, I believe." Combine this personality into a whole how you choose, it is certainly more than enough to furnish three ordinary women ; and, as a writer in the *New Statesman* recently suggested, it is, in this unmusical country, her personality almost as much as her music which has gained her honours—her D.B.E. in 1922, and even her festival in 1933. She may not have liked to be told so, but she would certainly see the joke. For one of her most characteristic traits is a splendid ability to see a joke against herself.

Ethel Smyth was born at Sidcup in Surrey about 1858. She was the fourth in a family of eight, six daughters and two sons, of whom one died young as the result of an accident. Of the daughters, all except Ethel married. Her father was an ex-officer of the Indian Army who settled down as an English country gentleman, first in Surrey and then at Frimley near Aldershot, and her mother a beautiful girl, half French by extraction and wholly French in education. There are unforgettable passages in the daughter's reminiscences describing Mrs. Smyth, her looks, her eager impulsiveness, her musical gifts, and her loving but tempestuous disposition, which could not prevent her quarrelling with her children, but was apt to rouse her to a mood of repentance early in the morning, when she would visit them in their bedrooms with anxious apologies. It is to be feared that the children, not so sensitive to the squabbles as their mother, and also at that time of day very sleepy, did not appreciate these visits as much as they were intended to.

They were a loud, boisterous, and turbulent family, of the kind of which one reads in Victorian novels, always getting into scrapes, being pursued by irate gardeners, quarrelling violently with one another, and generally making the lives of their successive governesses a burden to them.

The Smyths, like others of the heroines of this book, were educated, at any rate in their early years, by that Victorian phenomenon, the " resident governess "—and really, looking back on the time of our grandmothers, I am not sure that the " governesses " were not the oddest and the most pathetic thing about it. Governesses generally had no qualifications, or very few, and were not expected to have any. Generally they were supposed to be able to speak and write French and German, and to teach drawing ; as to other subjects—history, geography, arithmetic, and all the things that fill a schoolgirl's time to-day—it depended entirely upon the individual governess whether her pupils were taught them or not, and if they were, how well they were taught. For there was, in many cases, extraordinarily little supervision by the parents of what was taught ; the governess was judged much

DAME ETHEL SMYTH.

more according to whether she could keep the children in order or not. In the case of the Smyth family, which, as I have said, was vigorous and turbulent, the majority of governesses were found wanting ; at all events, Ethel's reminiscences record an endless succession of unfortunate women, passing through the schoolroom, all incompetent, all despised, and all bullied and plagued by the children. One wonders what became of all these poor and worthy women whose efforts were so useless ; it is comforting to think that nowadays, in houses where governesses are still employed, they are expected to have real qualifications, their work is treated seriously, and there is at any rate the beginnings of provision for their old age. But in the eighteen-sixties it was not so. Girls of the " respectable " classes were educated for the purpose of getting married and thereafter for fulfilling the enormous round of social duties—one can hardly call most of them pleasures—which women like Florence Nightingale found so desperately boring ; and that was that. Not that the governesses were any particular use even for that form of education. If you turn to the life of Clare Sheridan in this book you will find proof enough of that.

Ethel Smyth at all events learned little enough from her governesses, except that one of them wore false hair. She learned rather more from a school in Putney, to which she and her elder sister were sent in 1872 ; it was considered by her parents to be sufficiently respectable, as it was kept by the ex-governess of an old friend, and included among its pupils the daughter of a baronet and the daughters of two Honourables. There she was taken to see the Royal Academy and to hear Adelina Patti sing, neither of which experiences she could remember in later life ; but the principal piece of knowledge, according to herself, which she gained at school was how to darn stockings and to put clean linen at the bottom of the pile. Useful knowledge, no doubt, but it sounds an expensive way of acquiring it. For the rest, she learned her Bible from her family, Shakespeare from an aunt, and also undertook such varied experiences as riding a black pig bareback round the yard for the sum of sixpence, dressed in a clean white starched frock. It is not perhaps surprising that this last adventure ended in a spill into a manure-heap, and a penitential visit, all coated in manure, to General Smyth's study. He was, as I have said already, an old-fashioned father !

She was then not in any sense of the term a musical prodigy, as Mozart was, for example, and in early years, though obviously " musical," neither she nor any one else appears to have given her music much thought. But before the family moved to Frimley in 1867, she and her sister were singing duets—*i.e.* songs to which Ethel put " seconds " and accompaniments—and she made her first public appearance at a village concert at the age of eleven. By the time she was twelve the decision of her life had been made, and the agency of it, curiously enough, was one of the governesses whose ministrations and attainments she so heartily despised. In 1870 there arrived a new governess who had studied music at the Leipzig Conservatorium. From her Ethel heard for the first time of the delights of classical music, and shortly afterwards a friend gave her Beethoven's Sonatas to study for herself. Then and there her mind was made up, and she announced her intention of going to Leipzig and giving up her life to music. Naturally, nobody took this seriously ; it seemed a lunatic dream for a child of twelve, and especially for a female child of twelve, to think of giving up her life to music. But the decision was made, and she herself, as she tells us, never had any doubt that the dream would come to pass. There were, however, some years and many difficulties in the way. In 1875, after her elder sister Mary left school in order to " come out," Ethel, who was miserable at staying there without her, was allowed to leave, her next sister being sent in her place ; and almost immediately she became the eldest child at home, for two sisters married simultaneously and a few days afterwards her elder brother died after long ill-health. Now, it seemed, Ethel was all set to " come out," *i.e.* to make formal appearances in society, at dinner parties which she enjoyed heartily, taking care that after dinner nobody should get to the piano before her, lest her ears should be ravaged by their false or flat notes ; or at balls, which she enjoyed very much less, partly because her hair would not stay put up, and before the end of the evening always resembled the

head-dress of a Red Indian chief. Girls of this generation
do not realize one horror from which modern hair
fashions have saved them : the nightmare of having, at
the unskilful age of eighteen, to wind, and fasten in
position on top of one's head, long and heavy strands of
hair, in such a way that they would survive several hours
of the hopping and jumping involved in Victorian dances,
with curved instruments called hairpins sticking their
points into ears and scalp, and in extremity cascading all
over the floor. Some girls were naturally skilled at
" doing their hair " ; others could never learn, and most
were very inefficient at the time of their first ball. At
least two of the eminent women in this book, Dr. Smyth
and Mrs. Sidney Webb, never learned how to do their
hair.

Then, within a year or two, it was assumed, Ethel
would be presented to her Sovereign at one of the Royal
Drawing-rooms where the seal of respectability was put
on society young ladies, and she would thereafter take
up the county round as her mother's eldest daughter,
unless she rapidly followed her elder sisters into matrimony. She was actually, in fact, once engaged, to one
Wilfrid Wilde, brother of Oscar Wilde. Wilfrid Wilde
made her an impassioned proposal, with real Irish
eloquence, while she was being very sea-sick on a rough
passage of St. George's Channel ; but in spite of the
determination which this showed it does not seem to
have been a very serious affair on either side. The young

gentleman insisted on its being kept a secret : the young
lady in less than three weeks had broken off the engagement, asking to be allowed to keep the ring as a souvenir—
which she did until she lost it in a dog-fight a year or two
later. This was Ethel Smyth's sole venture in the direction
of matrimony ; the rest of the " young lady's " programme
was not fulfilled at all.

The main reason for this was the appearance, in the
Army Service Corps at Aldershot, of a Mr. Ewing, composer of the hymn *Jerusalem the Golden*, and husband of
Juliana Horatia Ewing. *Jerusalem the Golden* may not be
a staggeringly great piece of music, but it was one of the
most popular of the hymn tunes which were the only
kind of music that was not, at that time, seriously suspected of being frivolous and immoral ; and Mr. Ewing
was actually a very talented and enthusiastic amateur
musician. And Mrs. Ewing, the " Aunt Judy " who
wrote many charming children's books, *Jackanapes, Mary's
Meadow, The Great Adventure*, which, alas ! are now
almost entirely forgotten, was a most delightful personality, with whom Ethel instantly fell in love, and who
—which was perhaps more immediately useful—endeared
herself at the same time to General and Mrs. Smyth.
Some of Mrs. Ewing's letters make fascinating reading,
in spite of—or is it because of ?—the many references to
her " poor head," her " wretched spine," etc., which
run through them. Mrs. Ewing really did " enjoy poor
health," an occupation which is less fashionable now

13

than it used to be in the days of Dickens's Mrs. Gum-midge.

Ethel made friends with the Ewings, and Mr. Ewing, on discovering her musical leanings, demanded to hear her play and to see her compositions. Immediately he proclaimed that she was a born musician, and ought to be properly educated. And he suggested that he himself should begin by giving her lessons in harmony.

Then the fat was in the fire. The General, who, with all his merits, was in many ways not unlike the sort of father one finds depicted in Victorian novels, began to champ and roar. For all Ethel's reiteration of her desire for a musical career, he had never regarded it as a thing to be seriously contemplated—that she should go and live by herself in a foreign town and *study*. And he realized that the backing of one who was himself a musician was turning the project into a real possibility. Besides, it was not as if he liked the man. Mr. Ewing was not, un-fortunately, a man who dressed himself tidily. Also, he had a red nose—which the General always insisted was due to drink—and his manners were not always perfect. Influenced by his wife, the General gave way over the harmony lessons ; but had it not been for Mrs. Ewing's tact there would have been a family explosion then and there. Even so, his discovery, by searching in Ethel's desk—Victorian parents thought this quite a proper thing to do—of a passionate letter from Ewing exalting the glories of the musical life caused the harmony

lessons to come to an abrupt end. Shortly afterwards
the Ewings left Aldershot, but not before Ethel had made
the acquaintance of Aunt Judy's brother, the song-
writer A. S. Gatty, who warned her (no doubt meaning it
kindly) against " aiming too high " as a composer.

And now the time was coming for Ethel to be presented at the Queen's Drawing-room. During the inter-
vening months she had been confirming her musical
aspirations in one way and another, reading books on
music, attending concerts when she could, and on one
occasion being introduced to Frau Schumann, the widow
of the great composer ; and it so happened that on the
first day on which the subject of the Drawing-room was
definitely discussed she had for the first time heard the
Liebeslieder Waltzes of Brahms, who became one of the
great loves of her musical life. This may have given her
even more resisting power than usual ; at all events, when
the discussion began she proclaimed abruptly that it
would be no use to present her at any Drawing-room at all,
since she was going to study music at Leipzig whatever
anybody said, and even if she had to starve when she got
there.

It is probably difficult for people of this generation
to realize how appalling a prospect this seemed to General
Smyth ; it was worse than going on the stage would
have been in an earlier day. He knew no people who
lived by the practice of any art ; even the detested Mr.
Ewing was at least a soldier by profession and a musician

only in his spare time. If he thought about musicians at all, it was as people who habitually broke all the ten commandments, and he was probably quite serious in declaring that he would sooner see his daughter dead than studying music in Leipzig.

However, it did not quite come to that. Ethel, after vain arguments and storms and tempests of the kind which are apt to develop when an ex-General of the Indian Army finds himself divided on what he believes to be a question of principle and morality from his own daughter of eighteen, adopted a method which, if she had been brought up in the Labour movement, she would have called " the stay-in strike." She determined to make herself so unpleasant at home that in despair she would be sent away. She refused to co-operate in any way in the household : she would not sing at parties or go to church ; she would lock herself in her room. More than that, she would sneak out and up to London to go to concerts, borrowing the money from the trades-men of the neighbourhood—a scandalous thing to do—and travelling by third class and bus—all this in the days when a respectable English young lady was hardly sup-posed to go about by herself at all, and certainly not in a bus !

It could not go on ; friends intervened. A German singer, Fräulein Friedlander, was able to provide the name of an intensely respectable Frau Professor Heimbach who would be willing to take Ethel as a lodger in Leipzig,

16

and eventually the parental opposition crumbled. On July 26, 1877, Ethel Smyth, escorted by her brother-in-law Harry Davidson, set out for Germany.

.   .   .   .

She was now self-confessed and accepted as a serious student of music ; but it still remained to be seen whether there was the real stuff in her, and whether those who counted in the musical world would think so. For Mr. Ewing, if he was a gifted amateur, was after all only an amateur ; and it is a commonplace that amateurs are very ready to make their duck-like friends into swans. But in Germany she would be able with little delay to get at the opinion of those who really counted.

Some delay there had to be ; for in her eager desire to take advantage of her father's yielding she had omitted to make any inquiries about the dates of study in the Leipzig Conservatorium, and accordingly when she and Harry Davidson arrived in Leipzig they found that its doors would not be open for another month. Yet that was not disastrous, for she had time to wander about and get her bearings in Leipzig, and, even more effective, to go with some singers who were friends of hers to stay in a small wooden house on the edge of the Thuringian Forest, where they were later to be joined by the great baritone, himself a composer, Georg Hentschel.

The musical Germany into which Ethel Smyth stepped in 1877 was not present-day Germany. It was not even the Germany which those of us who are middle-

aged were taught to fear and hate from the reign of
Edward VII. onwards. There were exceptions ; the
policy of Bismarck, the Iron Chancellor who made the
little states into a German Empire dominated by the
Prussians, was beginning to have its effects, and some
Germans were already beginning to feel that hatred of
England which culminated in the European War nearly
forty years later. But in the main it was the Germany of
Goethe and Heine—the Germany, in fact, which most
people mean when they talk about the beauty of German
literature or even of German music. It was a Germany
of small states each of which had its own capital—as it
might be an English county-town—and its own constitution, its own dialect, and customs of its own, even, in
many cases, its own little court with its own little royalties,
all with their pedigrees traced in Debrett, and as proud as
though they had been kings of France. The Nazis have
swept all this away : they have destroyed the little courts
and the constitutions, thrown out Jewish artists such as
Mendelssohn was, and enthroned Wagner as the chief
composer of the new era instead of the Brahms and
Schumann whom Ethel Smyth loved ; but what the
effect will be on German music remains to be seen.

For there is no doubt that, whether or no the existence
of small states and tiny courts is politically a good thing,
it is a great assistance to music, even among a people
so naturally musical as the Germans are compared with
us. The English, since the seventeenth century, have

almost entirely ceased to be musical. We do not sing, except hymns. Try to teach any normal company of people a song whose tune is any more difficult than *The British Grenadiers*—or, worse still, try and get them to sing a song in parts—and see what a hash they make of it. We do not play instruments, not because we cannot do so, because it is generally agreed that the technical accomplishment of English professional orchestral players is among the best in the world (and so it needs to be, seeing with how little rehearsing they are generally expected to perform), but, presumably, because we do not want to. Since the arrival of piano players we do not even play the piano. What we do is to turn on the wireless or a gramophone, generally doing something else such as talking to friends, eating dinner, or preparing homework at the same time. Very occasionally we go to a concert or opera, which is unlikely to pay the promoters unless it is fashionable like Covent Garden or Glyndebourne, or made popular by the presence of a star singer singing the same song half a dozen times over, as a crowd will pack the Albert Hall to hear Tauber sing *You are my heart's delight*, without listening to anything else on the programme.

But even this unmusical nation would hear and produce more music if there were keen competition between all the counties and the chief towns to have good music and good musicians ; if Exeter, Birmingham, Hull, Winchester, Oxford, and the rest maintained Opera and Concert Houses, town orchestras and permanent musical directors, all vying with one another to obtain good new music for their particular towns.

In Germany this was the case, and had been the case since the Reformation if not before. Breslau, Leipzig, Dresden, Munich—to name only a few—all had their public orchestras and schools of music as well as Berlin ; and many of the small royal families maintained their own *Konzertmeister* or *Kapellmeister* or whatever he might be called, with his own musicians. You can read what this meant to music in the lives of any of the great German musicians such as Bach or Handel. It was, at least, the regular custom, at the time when Ethel Smyth was studying there, for contracts to be made for the production of a new work consecutively in three or four towns, which gave the public a real chance of finding out whether they liked it or not. Nor did the fact that it was a " flop " in the first town (if it was) necessarily discourage the others ; rather it stimulated them to go ahead and make it a success if they could. " They couldn't do anything with X's first Symphony in Munich," would have been a typical remark ; " it wasn't till it came to us that it really got across."

This kind of arrangement makes an enormous difference to music and to musicians, for most people do not realize—though they could if they stopped to think— what tremendous difficulties a composer of big works has to face before they can be known. A writer of all artists has perhaps the least troublesome time ; his materials are cheap and easily obtained, and if he can use a type-writer he needs no co-operation from anybody else in putting his work into the form in which a publisher can look at it. And when the book is published—and there are really a great many possible publishers—it is not gone from him. He can have as many copies as he likes to give to friends who missed it on its first appearance, or to show to publishers who might commission him to write another.

A painter is less fortunate. His materials are dearer, and his painted picture once it is sold is departed. He cannot both sell his picture and keep it to admire or to exhibit. A sculptor is perhaps less fortunate still. But both painter and sculptor can at least get their works photo-graphed and show the photographs to others ; and gener-ally if they want to put a particular picture or sculpture into a particular exhibition, they can borrow it temporarily—at least, if it has not been bought by the Melbourne or some equally distant Art Gallery.

But a composer ! First, before any considerable piece of music can be performed at all a hall must be provided, an orchestra be found, and that orchestra rehearsed as much as is possible. And, before they can even begin rehearsing, their parts must be copied out for them, either (as too often happens) by the composer himself with much labour, or by paid or more often underpaid music copyists, who are quite apt to make all sorts of mistakes. As musical items (except well-known operas) are not expected to have " runs " like plays, this means that no production of a new musical work can possibly be expected to pay, unless a very popular conductor such as Joachim or Toscanini can be persuaded to include it in his programme. It is illuminating to learn that when Ethel Smyth's Mass was performed in 1893 for the first time— it waited thirty-one years for a repetition—Messrs. Novello offered to bear the cost of the performance if Queen Victoria could be persuaded to attend. Hearing that this was out of the question, but that the Empress Eugénie, widow of Napoleon III., who was a friend of Ethel Smyth's, might possibly come, they replied that thàt would be very nice, but if it were only the Empress they could only guarantee half the cost. As Queen Victoria's musical appreciation was about on a level with that of the most unmusical of her subjects, and as the Empress on one occasion mistook *Partant pour la Syrie* for *God Save the Queen*, one may guess how much artistic weight the attendance of either of these distinguished ladies should really have carried.

Finally, the Mass or the Symphony, or whatever it is, having been once performed, what happens to it then ? It has not been printed or published, only written down in a number of single copies for individual performers. Printing of great orchestral scores is very expensive, and no music publisher is likely to undertake it except for a piece which has been a howling success. The text of the composition is practically lost ; sometimes, indeed, it is actually lost, as a work of Dr. Vaughan Williams was lost. And you cannot take photographs of a musical composition. What you *can* do, no doubt, is to make gramophone records ; but that, too, is expensive. Sir Thomas Beecham once wanted to make a Smyth Record Album ; but on investigation the composer found that it would cost her £500, which she did not happen to have " by her " at the moment. This was not so very long ago, and it is safe to say that no writer as well known as Ethel Smyth was then would have had to pay a penny, let alone £500, to get a book of his published. Mr. Gatty may have been wise, as well as depressing, in suggesting to her that she should write songs, which are comparatively cheap to print.

However, knowledge of this gloomy prospect was all before her when she arrived at Leipzig ; at the moment she had come to see whether real musicians, in a really musical country, thought anything of her ability. And immediately she reaped her reward for her obstinacy at home. Herr Hentschel, who, hearing that she composed, asked her in a momentary impulse of kindness to show him some of her work, not imagining, as he afterwards confessed, that there would be anything in it to interest him particularly, was completely taken by surprise, and said things that might well have turned the head of any girl of nineteen who had not a real passion for her art. He said "it was simply wonderful " ; and he would not

believe that she had had no tuition.   And others said
that she was the most talented woman composer who
had ever been seen in Leipzig.   From Ethel's letters to her
mother in that year can be gathered (if, indeed, one could
not have guessed it) the wild exultation produced in her
by the knowledge that she might really be going to turn
out a swan in the end—exultation tempered by the
realization that this was only the beginning, that she must
work and work at her job if she was to be the composer
she now saw that she had a chance of becoming.

Then began eight years of almost pure excitement,
the sort of excitement which all young persons of genius
experience when they first realize that the genius is there,
and that all the work that they can do will be really
useful and productive in bringing it to perfection.   Also,
it was Germany, with all the music to hear and to play,
and all the musicians to meet—a glorious prospect for
anybody so naturally enthusiastic.   She met Frau
Schumann again ; she met Lili Wachs, the brilliant and
sensitive daughter of Mendelssohn ; she met, above all,
the beautiful Elizabeth von Herzogenburg, wife of a
distinguished composer and friend of Brahms, whose
passionate friend she almost immediately became.   After
Frau von Herzogenburg, in the following spring, had
nursed her through a serious illness brought on simply
by overwork and over-intoxication with music and with
Germany, she became her husband's pupil, and thereafter
for several years was a kind of semi-detached member of

their household, until unfortunately her friendship with Elizabeth came to a tragic end. She also met Brahms ; but, much as she admired his music, one does not get the impression that she was perfectly at home with the man himself. She did not like his manners—in which view, indeed, she was not alone ; Brahms was one of the rudest of men. And she detested his attitude to women, or rather *Weibsbilder*. (The word is almost untranslatable ; it conveys the impression of woman as a useful object, part of the furnishings of the home. No wonder it infuriated Ethel Smyth.)

All this was not secured or enjoyed without a certain amount of inconvenience. For one thing, she was not at all well off. It is true that her father, once he had given in, made her an allowance—if he had not, it would have been impossible for her to live in Leipzig at all ; but he had many children, and he was not a provident man, and her allowance was not by any means munificent. Sometimes she was hard put to it to get along at all. In 1881 Von Herzogenburg told her, a propos of some touring experience, that whenever she came to a town her instinct was to make for the most unprepossessing hotel she could find and ask it for a *Kutscher Zimmer*, which means a " cabman's room." At that age, any one who has the salt of the earth in them ought to prefer adventure-with-cheapness to comfort, but the general straitness of her finances may have had something to do with her choice.

There were also, however, certain difficulties connected with being an unattached young female in a
German town in the seventies. Almost immediately
upon her arrival in Leipzig she desired to go to a concert
in the Rosenthal Restaurant, at which a Serenade of
Hoffmann's was to be performed, but her landlady told
her that a young girl could not conceivably go alone,
and that therefore she would have to miss it, as she
herself would be engaged that night on the *Grosse Wäsche*,
i.e. the monthly ceremony at which all the dirty linen
of the household was washed. On this occasion the
problem was solved by Ethel's hiring corkscrew grey curls
and a pair of horn-rimmed spectacles, borrowing from
the old lady a veil and a gown (which pads of folded
newspaper made into an excellent fit), and taking with
her a piece of knitting as a final *alibi*. But for the most
part she had to rely upon the reputation of the English
for lunacy to keep her out of scrapes, and to enable her
to climb unmolested into her lodging over a seven-foot
wooden paling, when—as happened more than once—
she had left behind the enormous rusty key which
opened it.

Nevertheless, as I have said, the seven or eight years
which followed her introduction to Germany were a
very happy time. She was learning ; she had many
friends ; she returned to England at intervals, where she
could hunt and play tennis and see her family ; she was
beginning to get her works performed ; and she went to

Italy, and went mountaineering, a sport which intoxicated her nearly as much as hunting. Even after the bitter break with Elizabeth von Herzogenburg, which occurred in 1885 and poisoned, for the time being at least, many of her German relationships, she did not abandon Germany, until in 1889, ill and unhappy in Munich in spite of her successes, she came home to Frimley, to her parents. Her mother died, somewhat unexpectedly, little more than a year later, and her father in 1894, after which the house at Frimley was sold ; and Ethel, having bought from the sale, among other things, the old schoolroom table under which her brother Johnny had crouched while she and her sister threw knives at each other, took up her abode, protected by an enormous and alarming dog called Marco and an old servant of her mother's called Ford, in a small property known as One Oak—presumably because there were several other oaks in the neighbourhood.

.   .   .   .

This is not a life of Ethel Smyth, but a sketch of the formative influences which made her into the woman and composer she afterwards became. We need not, therefore, hunt for details of all her life, which has included friendships with people like Lady Ponsonby (mother of the present Lord Ponsonby) and the Empress Eugénie, productions of her works in Germany and in England (alas ! many too few in this country, though the Smyth Festival, held in 1933, may perhaps be considered as a partial

27

amendment), violent interludes like her militant suffrage activities between 1911 and 1913, and honours such as the D.B.E., given her in 1922, and a Doctorate of Music received in 1928 from Durham University, at the instigation, so she tells us, of a Canon who years before had watched her playing tennis from behind a curtained window—whether it was the music or the tennis that had impressed him will probably never be known. It remains to inquire why a composer of the energy and ability of Ethel Smyth has not become better known—or rather, more frequently heard—in her own country.

It would not be very sensible for one as comparatively ill-educated in music as the present writer to attempt to fix Ethel Smyth's position among the world's composers. Suffice it to say that whenever I have heard her music—music such as *The Wreckers*—I have been convinced that it is the kind of music which ordinary people could like and understand, if they were given a chance. On the whole, I think it is true to say that they have not been given very much chance. As previously explained, in this country new music must commend itself to a few influential people if it is to be performed at all. Ethel Smyth's own belief is that those few influential people dislike her work and will not make any effort to get it produced. She further believes—being a strong feminist—that there is a real unwillingness to consider that a woman can compose anything worth hearing, and instances a famous conductor, Hermann Levi, who after hearing a choral work of hers, said, " I could never

have believed that a woman wrote that." "No," said
she, "and what is more, in a week's time you won't
believe it!" and if Ethel Smyth is a good witness, he
accepted those words as a fair score. As to that, it is
difficult to say : there have been so few women, whether
in England or anywhere else, who even attempted to
make themselves felt as composers. In the meantime
one can only urge any one who is at all interested in
music to take any opportunity that offers itself of listening
to any music of Ethel Smyth's, wherever they can find it,
and to form their own opinion for themselves. At present
there is only one English composer of opera who can be
sure of a hearing, anyhow and anywhere, and that is the
composite body called Gilbert and Sullivan. While
nobody would deny the merits of Sullivan's music when
combined with Gilbert's words (though not by itself), it
seems a little unfortunate that real popular appreciation of
British operatic music should have stopped with Sullivan's
death.

LADY HENRY SOMERSET

II

LADY HENRY SOMERSET

IN March 1921 an old lady of seventy died after two days' illness. Few people at the time of her death remembered that that little old lady had once moved in the highest society in the country : perhaps even fewer that she had been a public figure whose eloquence drew great audiences in the United States, who wrote important letters to the *Times*, and who had been the centre of violent controversy. For many years before her death she had devoted herself quietly to her own particular charity, which, valuable as it was—as we shall see—was not of the kind which makes a great stir in the world. And yet the reading of that little old lady's life is of considerable interest, because it shows so clearly both out of what vigorous and obstreperous stock the great families of Victorian England came and what an extraordinarily unsuitable training and education was imposed upon their younger members when they had become respectable. Lady Henry Somerset managed to survive the idiocies of her education, and in the end to build a fine and useful character out of it ; but every one who reads her life must realize how much of her energy was wasted, and how much unnecessary suffering she went through because of her upbringing.

To understand the story we must begin far back. It is fairly often remarked that, if you go back far enough into the ancestry of the most respectable English families, you will find extremely disreputable characters. In the case of Lady Henry Somerset it is not necessary to go back very far before finding something which is at any rate dubious. Her grandfather was a Mr. James Pattle, who married a Frenchwoman, daughter of the Chevalier Antoine de l'Etang, who had been page to Marie Antoinette, the Queen of France who perished in the Revolution. Mr. James Pattle was " a rich Bengal merchant," and any one who knows anything of the early history of the English merchants in India, before that country was brought directly under the rule of the Crown, will realize that Bengal merchants became rich rather by force of character (not to say cunning) than by adherence to the strict principles of morality. Mr. James Pattle, at all events, was known to his enemies as " the biggest liar in India," and to his friends, more mildly, as " Jim Blazes."

When he died in India, it was found that he had left instructions that his body was to be taken home to England and buried with his forefathers. Accordingly, the corpse was packed in a cask of spirits of wine—the only way known at that time of preserving it for the long journey—and Mrs. Pattle, with her two youngest daughters, embarked it and themselves on a ship for England. But before they had gone very far there was a violent storm ; the cargo was flung hither and thither in the hold, the top of the cask was knocked off, and Mr. Pattle, embalmed and stiff, appeared in the opening. The poor widow, called in to see the sight and to identify her husband, went out of her mind with the shock of it and died raving mad.

Curiously enough, this story of Jim Pattle was a favourite of General Smyth, father of Ethel Smyth, who also figures in this book. He used to tell it in a somewhat more dramatic form, adding, among other refinements, that after the storm the ship ran upon a rock and drifted ashore on the Hoogly River, and that the sailors said that Pattle had been such a scamp that the devil would not let him go out of India. Whichever version one accepts, it is clear enough that Mr. James Pattle was a considerable scamp, and also a violent egotist who bullied his wife and his subordinates, and had plenty of character.

As sometimes seems to happen in the case of men of exceptionally violent and obstreperous dispositions, James Pattle had no sons. The name Pattle therefore disappears, and the disposition is left to the charge of seven daughters. Not that they were unworthy guardians. They were all beautiful, all full of vitality, all devoted to one another, careless of fashion—in the middle of the Victorian age they refused to wear corsets or crinolines, and sat up all night in one another's houses, chattering in Hindustani and making themselves gorgeous clothes in which they walked magnificently through the streets of London. Also they were self-willed, strong minded, and recklessly generous, whether with their own or with other people's money. "Julia," said the patient tongue of the husband of one of them, Charles Cameron of Lochiel, "Julia is carving up Ceylon again," when his wife's philanthropic activities reduced him to selling some of his estates there.

Seven of them there were, and the youngest was Virginia, the most beautiful and not by any means the least vigorous. Her portrait was painted for the Royal Academy (and on many other occasions) by G. F. Watts, who was already famous when he saw her walking down the street and demanded to be introduced. But either Mr. Watts idealized the young Miss Pattle to excess or she had already learned that the business of a Victorian young lady in society was not to look strong minded, however strong minded she might be ; for nobody would guess, from looking at the demure, mild expression of the face in the portrait, the long soft lines, and the gentle colours, that any of the fire of old Jim Blazes lay underneath. Nor, though the portrait led to her wedding, did it give her future husband much of an idea of her character.

The circumstances of that wedding were rather romantic, in the story-book sense. A young man called

Charles Somers-Cocks, who was also Viscount Eastnor and came of the best English county families, desired above all things to become a painter ; but his mother, Countess Somers, who was shocked at the idea, explained to him that, while he might dabble in colour if he chose, it would never do for an English gentleman to paint like an artist. English gentlemen, if they insisted on painting, must at least paint badly, so as to show they need not do it for a living. So Charles Somers-Cocks, denied the joy of being a painter, wandered about looking at other people's paintings, and at the Royal Academy saw the portrait of Virginia Pattle, and considered that if he could not paint the original at least he could have it in his house. He proposed, and was accepted, and instantly passed from the domination of his mother to that of his wife. From the day of his marriage Viscount Eastnor —soon to become Earl Somers—ceased to possess a will of his own. He did not cease to have opinions, and some-times even to express them, and where they have been recorded as conflicting with those of his wife, his were generally right. But they never were of any effect against the immense humourless power of the daughter of Jim Blazes (wherever Lady Henry Somerset got her sense of humour from it was certainly not from her mother). However, he was a mild young man and tremendously in love with his beautiful and imperious wife, and perhaps he liked it. There seems no sign of serious discord, and certainly the Pattles, most of whom married men of social standing whom they consistently controlled, must have been a formidable family to be connected with.

There were three children of the marriage : Isabel, born in 1851, Adeline, born in 1852, and Virginia, born in 1853. Virginia, whom Isabel remembered vaguely as " the naughtiest child that ever lived "—obviously a true Pattle—died of neglected diphtheria when she was quite young while her mother was abroad, and the fear of death which that engendered in Lady Somers probably intensified her determination to bring up her two remaining children in a strict and almost savage retirement. I do not mean to imply that they were ill-treated—not in the least ; only that they were well treated and everlastingly looked after in an atmosphere of such seclusion, such restrictions, and such endless fussing as would drive a modern child nearly off its head. Poor little Isabel, at the age of five, told a friend that she would be " quite happy if I had not so many relations " ; and that about expresses the situation. They were guarded like egg shells that would break at a touch, and simultaneously trained with steady severity in the knowledge and accomplishments thought to be necessary for the great position in the world that was to be theirs—trained, in fact, in everything but any experience of the world whatsoever.

We do not know how Lady Somers got into her head this idea about her children's upbringing, for it certainly did not resemble her own, which had been far freer, both in India under her French mother and her scandalous

father, and subsequently in England while she and her
sisters were defying the fashions. The death of Virginia
may, as I have suggested, have had something to do with
it, but the system had begun in some form long before
that. When Isabel was not yet five her mother was already
commenting, in letters to friends, upon the qualities
of the *seventh* nursery governess and her probable inade-
quacy for her task—for the governesses were supervised
quite as severely as the children. Perhaps she had an
obscure feeling that the Pattle blood was too violent, and
that unless it was trained to be good and dull it would
break out disastrously. But more probably it was due
as much as anything to an unconscious desire not to let
the children grow up and to be troubled with the problems
of their growing up, to keep them as long as possible
tender, protected babies, and to an obstinate unimagina-
tiveness that absolutely refused to see into what a dismal
régime she was cramping them, and how sharply it must
contrast with her own. Whatever the cause was, it was
not lack of affection. Wherever she went and whatever
she was doing, it is plain from her letters that her " March
lambs," as she called her daughters, were constantly in
her thoughts, and she was continually writing to them
and determining their welfare.

Consider for a moment the actual life they led.
Whether their parents were at home or away, they were
kept in the schoolroom, and under the immediate care
and instruction of governesses, who succeeded one another

in rapid succession. Isabel, in her schoolroom life, experienced no less than twenty of these, so difficult was it to satisfy Lady Somers—and at the end of it all she could not even spell decently. Not that spelling was their only subject of instruction, or that they were not worked pretty hard. Here is the programme of a single day for Isabel : 9.30 to 10, German translation ; 10 to 10.30, practising ; 10.30 to 11, learn German poetry ; 11 to 11.30, music lesson ; 11.30 to 12, read German ; 1.15 to 1.45, lie flat and learn *Chambers's Questions* (a sort of enormous series of General Knowledge papers which asked you, " What is the date of the Armada ? Where is Buda-Pesth ? What is bread made of ? " and so on) ; 4.30 to 5.30, lie flat and hear Greek history read aloud ; 5.30 to 6.30, write German letter ; 6.30 to 7, singing. Another day would be a " French day," with a nearly similar programme ; and of course there was also Scripture and drawing and perhaps a little botany ; but of subjects which girls at school to-day enjoy, hardly anything. It makes one indignant to think that six and a half hours of precious time could be so wasted and so boring.

They were not, of course, learning German or French or practising all the time. What did they do with the rest of it ? On some afternoons they went for a drive in the carriage with the governess ; on others they rode on horseback with a groom—one at a time, for they were not allowed to ride together lest they should get over-

[*Elliott and Fry.*

LADY HENRY SOMERSET.

excited. Nor were they allowed to ride on two afternoons in succession. At 12 o'clock, generally, when they were at Eastnor Castle or one of their other homes, they were allowed to walk in the garden ; but even that was strictly regulated, for Isabel, during a hot summer, writes to her mother pleading for leave to go into the garden after breakfast, " as at 12 o'clock it is so Boiling." They did sewing for the poor, and embroidery : their governesses read aloud to them, and they were ordered to read for themselves.

But not to read freely—oh, dear, no. Once, in an incautious letter to her mother, the Lady Isabel let out that the Lady Adeline had been reading a novel called *Mrs. Haliburton's Troubles*, by Mrs. Henry Wood, who was an immensely popular author in the latter half of the nineteenth century. Back instantly came a storm of reproaches, and instructions not to read *any* novel unless it be one by Miss Charlotte Yonge or Miss Sewell (authoress of *Black Beauty*) or Sir Walter Scott—" but of *his*," she adds, " I do not wish you to read *any* but those you have read." At that Lord Somers made a mild protest—he said in effect that the books which were permitted to children were sentimental rubbish and gave them a false and foolish view of life. But Lady Somers was quite unmoved : she was not afraid of sentimental rubbish, or of false views of life, only of dangerous ideas. Nevertheless, Isabel somehow managed to get hold of and to read John Stuart Mill's famous radical tract

On Liberty, which deeply influenced so many generations of reformers and even of Socialists. This, however, she was wise enough not to discuss with her mother. One cannot help realizing that, during all these years when she was shut up like a chicken in an incubator, there was developing in Isabel, underneath her expressed and real desire to be " good," in the sense in which her mother and her governesses interpreted it, a deep sense of justice and sympathy with the wrongs of human creatures, which, combined with the complete lack of any training for life, were to get her into great difficulties later on.

Such was their routine when they were at home and well, and few of those who saw them riding and driving in their beautiful clothes with their retinue of attendant servants, and thought how like fairy princesses they seemed, can have realized how intolerably narrow and dull, even for this period, their lives were. They had no friends ; they met no other children. Practically their sole entertainment was to visit the poor on the estates ; for, as to going to plays or concerts . . . When Isabel was nearly eighteen she was allowed, as a special treat and provided that she and her nurse-companion wrapped up " like mummies " and took the large carriage, to go down to the village night-school for a few minutes after dinner ! If they were at all ill, if one of them coughed or sneezed or had a headache or a backache, it was even worse ; for at the faintest hint of such a calamity they were hurried off, governess, maid, grooms, ponies, piano, and all, to some seaside place such as Brighton, Worthing, or Aberystwyth, where they pursued exactly the same régime as at home, save that the lodgings must have been less pleasant and more uncomfortable than Eastnor Castle, and they had no gardens to walk in. It cannot have been much like our idea of a seaside holiday, for they were followed by reams of letters, instructions, inquiries, parcels of food, etc. etc., and however weary they got of it and however much they longed to come back, there was no possibility of disobeying Lady Somers's instructions. One of the most serious scrapes into which Isabel got was when, she being nearly eighteen and her mother out of England, she had ventured upon a slight disarrangement of their summer plans. It is true that it was in order to do nothing more dangerous than to pay a visit to her aunt, her own mother's sister ; but the fact, when known at St. Moritz, where her mother was staying, brought down upon her head a whole spate of furious letters accusing her of intrigue, of self-will, and of giving way to " grave faults of character and principle."

It might have been less hard to bear if there had been nothing to contrast it with. Eastnor Castle and Reigate Priory were " great houses," homes of political and social importance, where a great deal of thrilling entertaining was always in progress, and where important and interesting people were always coming and going. Lady Somers herself lived a full and exciting life. People had admired and courted her for her spirit and beauty when she was

a girl ; when she was a married woman they admired
her no less, and eminent persons like Lord Lansdowne
told her Cabinet secrets or semi-secrets, discussed poetry
with her, and asked her advice.   Nor was she confined to
England, or to the society of England : nearly half the
year was commonly spent abroad, travelling to Italy,
France, or Greece, buying clothes in Paris or pictures in
Venice, or simply drifting about on long cruises in the
Mediterranean.   Many of Lady Somers's letters to her
" March lambs" were dispatched from foreign addresses,
and contained, amid all the exhortations to good conduct,
vivid descriptions of the beautiful country in which she
was at the moment staying ; and one can only conclude
that it must have been an extraordinarily unimaginative
parent to whom it never occurred that her children might
find the contrast between the gay and colourful life which
she was describing and their own rigidly circumscribed
existence too intolerable to be endured.   At any rate,
no reflection of this kind seems ever to have occurred to
their mother.

.   .   .   .

Even the most dreary childhood must come to an
end some time ; and at last, when she was a few months
short of nineteen, Lady Isabel was due to be " presented,"
that is to say, to leave the schoolroom and to burst upon
the world in the guise of a marriageable young lady.
Immediately this meant a long skirt—several long skirts,
in fact, as she must have a proper wardrobe—hair

elaborately dressed, and her removal from the régime of the schoolroom into a régime of parties and entertainments hardly less rigid and exacting, if more amusing. The pursuit of amusement, if sternly organized, can be quite as exhausting as the pursuit of knowledge. As another of our heroines, Beatrice Webb, discovered, a society season, when taken really seriously, left one ill and thoroughly dissatisfied at the end of it ; and though she was not perhaps as serious as Mrs. Webb, Isabel's letters to her sister, who was still in the schoolroom, do not by any means give the impression of unadulterated enjoyment. She is " crushed with fatigue." She is " too tired to write " ; she went to " an odious ball at Strawberry Hill yesterday "—even if some of this may be a little exaggerated in order to impress her junior, nevertheless there must have been some basis of fact for it. Nor was she, in fact, much freer of parental influence than she had been in the schoolroom ; she was very frightened, young, and unsure of herself (how indeed could she have been anything else ?), and she gave observers the impression of a young foal, running timidly at her mother's side and quite unaware of her own attractions.

On one disastrous occasion she did venture to speak up for herself. She had gone (with her mother) to a party at which they played round games in the evening. In one of the round games, called " Wishes," all the participants were required to say truthfully what was the dearest wish of their hearts. Isabel, when her turn came, said

eagerly, " To live in the country and to have fifteen children " ; and thought, from the applause which greeted
her, that her contribution had been a success. It was
only afterwards, when her mother scolded her cruelly
and declared that she had been covered with shame to
hear a daughter of hers express so unmaidenly a view,
that she realized anything was wrong. It seems rather
hard, when one considers that the whole training of
Isabel and Adeline Somers-Cocks was directed to making
them suitable girls for English country gentlemen to
marry, to make into mistresses of their English country
houses, and, it is to be supposed, mothers of their children
(even if fifteen was rather a large number !), that Isabel
should be so rated for putting this idea into words—but
people are not always logical.

All the same, whether or not it was proper for her
to say so, marriage was her destiny, the career for which
her mother intended her ; and married she was, before
she was twenty-one, to Lord Henry Somerset, the second
son of the Duke of Beaufort. If she had been free of her
mother's influence, and if (which is much more important) she had ever been in the slightest degree encouraged or habituated to judge people for herself, it is very
doubtful whether she would have chosen Lord Henry.
She had met other young men who—since she was a
very pretty lively girl—were inclined to pay court to
her ; towards one of them, Lord Lorne (son of the Duke
of Argyll), she seems to have entertained feelings of

affection. But whether or not Lord Lorne intended to propose to her, he never did (some said it was because of Queen Victoria, who had other plans for him*); and in despair of romance she decided only to marry a man who was " good," in the sense in which her childhood's reading had taught her to understand the word. Lord Henry Somerset, at that time, had leanings towards philanthropy, towards being " kind to the poor," which Isabel had always been taught was her duty ; being only a second son, he was neither very rich nor very important, but (which commended him to Lady Somers) he came of one of the " best " English families. Accordingly, in 1872, Isabel Somers-Cocks became Lady Henry Somerset. Her father disapproved ; but, as usual, he was overruled.

Immediately the result of her marriage was an enormous widening of her life and interests. From being a little foal, running at her mother's knee, she became a married woman of importance, with her own rooms and her own horses, and nobody to give her orders, so long as she kept on good terms with her husband's father and mother in their great house at Badminton in Wiltshire. This she found easy enough, particularly as the régime at Badminton did not at all closely resemble the strict rule under which she had been brought up. The household at Badminton belonged to an earlier type of English country house, in which the members were allowed to

* At any rate, he very soon married Princess Louise, the Queen's fourth daughter.

do pretty much what they liked, so long as they preserved certain decencies of outward behaviour, and the only rule which the Duchess of Beaufort enforced upon her daughter-in-law was that she should always wear white gloves, even in the house. Meantime, she had the chance of meeting on equal terms many of the most charming and entertaining persons of the day, and developing her own charm by contact with them.

But this interlude lasted for a comparatively little while. From every possible angle Lord Henry Somerset was a bad husband. That there is no doubt about his ill-treatment of his wife is proved by the fact that by 1877 his own father and mother were " bitterly grieved and ashamed " at his conduct, and were admitting as much to his wife. The birth of their son in 1874 had not brought any improvement.

In those days, and in high society in particular, it was not at all easy for a wife to get a divorce from her husband, however badly he behaved. In such circles as that of Badminton, married couples whose marriage had not turned out a success were supposed to grin and bear it, and particularly not to make a public to-do. However, it was possible for people quietly to separate from one another ; and probably that might have been the fortune of Lady Henry Somerset—who herself desired only to escape quietly—had not her humourless mother suddenly hurried home from one of her trips abroad, and persuaded herself that her daughter was in terrible danger

48

and must escape at once. So, on a night in 1878, Lady Henry, only half-dressed, ran away with her baby to her parent's house—and immediately found herself in serious trouble, because under the law of the land the baby belonged to his father. Eventually the problem was smoothed out, and the separation arranged, but not without a lawsuit and a great deal of publicity which was very distressing for Lady Henry, because a number of people who had hitherto been her friends leaped to the conclusion that as she had got mixed up with the law courts she must be a bad woman, and not suitable for them or their wives and children to meet. She was cut by acquaintances at the Opera ; men who met her told her that they could not introduce her to their wives ; and when her only sister married the son of the Duke of Bedford the mother-in-law refused to meet her. She was only twenty-seven.

There is no need to say more about the tragedy of Lady Henry's brief marriage. Its importance is not in itself, but because it cut her life in half. At one blow she was severed from the chief part of the society in which she had been popular and taken pleasure before, and thrown upon her own resources. No doubt there were some people who would have stood by her and remained her friends if she had sought them out. But she was proud ; she did not care to ask, and run the risk of being cut in public—as in fact happened to her at least once. She had not herself wished to create a public scandal ; that she had done so was the fault of her mother and her mother's ascendancy over her, and she wished, if possible, to forget about it. But if it had not happened, if Lady Henry had not felt, in her own life, what it was like to be an outcast, there would be no reason to be writing about her here. She had done nothing which she could herself consider wrong ; but she had become an outcast. What was she to do ?

.   .   .   .

For a time she did nothing spectacular, but lived comparatively quietly in the country. She had not, of course, been cut off from all her friends, only from the more important and straitlaced, and at Reigate Priory, a house of her father's to which she betook herself, she gathered from time to time a circle of friends which, while it was less exalted than that in which she had previously moved, and had what one might call a faint flavour of lack of respectability, nevertheless must have been freer for the mind, and even, it is possible, more amusing than the surroundings of her early life. At least the members of this circle were able openly to read John Stuart Mill and even Mrs. Henry Wood if they wanted to.

But it was not much of a life, and she knew it. Of two things she really felt the need. The first was to have some focus for the energies which the Pattle blood had bequeathed to her and which were no longer being consumed in the elaborate society round. And she had plenty of energy to be expended as recklessly as she did

her cash. The main result of the anxious care which her
mother had given to her health in youth was to make
her, when she grew up, entirely careless of it ; and as to
money, she had no more natural appreciation of it than
any of her relatives. Though in her diary she is frequently
scolding herself for not being properly attentive to the
questions of finance, we find again and again that her
sister has to come to her rescue in scrapes. Certainly the
vast estates of the Duke of Bedford, to whom her sister's
husband was heir, could stand the strain without noticing
it at all ; but one cannot feel that it would have made the
old Duchess of Bedford feel any more kindly to Lady
Henry.

Her other need was religion. As in the case of many
whose lives have met with disaster for reasons that they
cannot trace to faults in themselves, she felt desperately
the need of some faith which would enable her to believe
that the world was really all right, that there was some
fundamentally beneficent power in it which was working
to a pattern which could be understood, and which cared
for and sympathized with human suffering. Again and
again her diaries show her crying out for the knowledge
of a personal God who should give her this certainty,
and feeling that the Anglican religion of her childhood
was not enough, not personal enough, or strong or vivid.
She wanted something at once more vigorous and more
compelling.

As the years went on it seemed that she might be

finding an answer to both of her needs. She had begun, at Reigate Priory, to take an interest in the affairs of the estate and of the tenants, which fitted on to the only work of social value which had formed part of her training—that of visiting the poor—but here she was at first hampered by her lack of any other training at all. She could go to see the sick and take them soup and flowers, and she could also—not being quite blind—observe when it was clearly impossible that the sick could recover their health in the cottages in which they were compelled to live. But if it was suggested that they should have new cottages, then it became a matter for the estate accounts ; and poor Lady Henry, with no business training at all and very little natural aptitude for it, grappled with the mysteries of sand and gravel pits and what could be derived from them, of farming and stock accounts which never seemed to work out on the right side, until her head was in a whirl. Nor was her father, on that point, of much assistance ; for his interest in his estates was principally æsthetic, and he would order newly built stables to be pulled down at once on the ground that their appearance was unpleasing, which may have been artistic, but was expensive.

In 1883 Lord Somers died, and as he had no son, Lady Henry moved to Eastnor Castle in Herefordshire, the chief house of his estates, and prepared to take up her duties seriously as a landed proprietress. For the next seven years she lived there almost entirely without

the companionship of her own class, her chief human
contacts being with her own poor tenants and with the
little band of fervent Methodists who lived in the small
town of Ledbury. For a time she thought she had found
among them the quality of religion she had longed for,
in their fervent personal piety and in their steady care
for the poor creatures who lived in the wretched conditions of the Ledbury slums. She went to their meetings,
and spoke at them ; she prayed with them ; she established mission halls, both on her own property and elsewhere, at which she provided converted clowns to entertain the people and keep them out of the pubs ; and she
even—though with her upbringing and her natural love of
gaiety and entertainment it was quite a serious deprivation—eventually took the pledge herself because she felt
that it was impossible for her to go round Ledbury urging
poor men to keep out of public-houses if she herself took
a drink whenever she felt like it.

At the time, it should be remembered, the " evil of
drink " was a very much more serious problem in England
than it is to-day. Ever since the introduction in the
eighteenth century of unrestricted spirit-drinking, particularly of gin, sold in places which advertised that you
could get " drunk for a penny, dead-drunk for twopence ;
straw provided free," England had been, in comparison
with, say, France and Germany, a drunken country ;
and though restrictions had been introduced, there was
still a great deal of drinking which was in no sense

pleasurable or social, but simply entered upon as a way of forgetting for a while the intolerable conditions under which the drunkard lived—and in days when there were no cinemas, few entertainments, and little means of cheap transport by bus, etc., the public-house was often the *only* way of escape. When a contemporary social worker named Canon Barnett asked a man in Whitechapel whom he was trying to reform why he got drunk, the man's simple and devastating answer was that " Drink was the shortest way out of Whitechapel." But it was an expensive way, and a way that was apt to bear very hardly on the man's wife and children ; and it is not surprising that the nineteenth-century social workers, even when they believed that the only real remedy was to destroy Whitechapel and the living conditions of such places as Whitechapel altogether, also thought that, for the sake of those who were at the present time condemned to live in Whitechapel, the easy way out should be combated—and became, like Lady Henry, ardent temperance reformers. In Lady Henry's case, the call came to her more strongly because one of her dearest friends committed suicide under the influence of drink ; but even without that additional urge she would probably have taken up the cause.

Yet her life was not entirely satisfactory. With the natural sense of proportion and humour which in spite of her training never deserted her, she began to find the narrow definition of goodness preached by her Methodist friends impossible to endure. They were so censorious, so insistent that the lives of every one they deigned to admit as one of them should be conducted exactly on the lines they prescribed. They held inquisitions—there is no other word—on Lady Henry ; they thought she was frivolous, vain, and foolish ; they suspected her of all sorts of sins, and said so often in very harsh terms. Lady Henry was meek ; she agreed eagerly that she was frivolous and vain and foolish, and tried pathetically to overcome these faults. But when one earnest worker, who must have been an exceptionally unimaginative woman, had the cruelty to tell her that her son was her idol and that God would take him away from her, and that she would spend long months in agony—then she began to wonder whether she had been wise in so enthusiastically embracing her new friends. She had not —and never seems to have had—any conception of what curious forms jealousy and spite can take.

At the same time she was getting into trouble with the " County." The great ones of the neighbourhood approved of mild " slumming " on one's own property ; they did not approve of poking one's nose into conditions elsewhere. They approved of the poor being prevented from drinking ; they did not approve of their being entertained, certainly not by clowns, however fully converted. And when Lady Henry went on to investigate the conditions under which the people lived, which drove them to drink, indignation began to grow. One man complained that she " disfigured the countryside with new cottages " ; a lady who had known her from childhood sent for her and asked her if she realized that she was a traitor to her class. Nor were there wanting people who were ready to rake up her past history, and to murmur that nothing good could be expected of any one who had once got herself into trouble.

Nevertheless she continued to work ; she spoke at meetings, both on temperance and on social questions, as far afield as South Wales, and in 1890 she shared a plat-form in the East End with John Burns, the Labour leader. It was then that she met the lady to whom it is partly due that she became, for a short while, one of the best-known public figures in the United States.

Mrs. Pearsall Smith was an American. She was a member of the American Women's Temperance Associa-tion, whose secretary at the time was that eager, ardent, merciless prohibitionist Miss Frances Willard ; and she had come over to England with her family to stay for a while and to meet the members of the British Women's Temperance Association, which had itself been founded, about ten years previously, by an English Quaker lady who had been visiting the States. Lady Henry was already a fairly prominent member of the British society ; so that it was no casual chance which led her to meet Mrs. Pearsall Smith just before her East End meeting. But it led to an invitation to stay at Eastnor Castle, which about filled that lady's cup of delight.

For Mrs. Pearsall Smith was an American, very typical of many of her countrywomen, and that not only during the eighteen-eighties. She was, in the first place, extremely healthy, quite well-off, and thoroughly cheerful. It had never occurred to her that she could want anything she could not have, or fail to do anything on which she set her heart—or that anybody else could be in that position for any reason except lack of will or energy. If there was something that she could not by any means combat or get over she stared it in the face, and declared that it either did not exist or did not matter. When, for instance, her attention was directed to the slums and their effect on the drink trade, she remarked that she never worried about the slums, for they were " Heavenly Father's Housekeeping "—whatever that might mean ; and she was able to walk along the Westminster Embankment at night and look at the wretched homeless creatures who lay there with nothing but indignation for their improvidence, and no inquiries about how they had come to be in such a state. Such a useful thing it is to have a simple mind which can provide itself with blinkers when needed.

She was pleased with England, and happy in it, though, of course, convinced of the unquestioned superiority of America. Confronted at one meeting with some revelations of English social conditions, she wrote home, " I cannot think that those old nations in the land of Canaan, the Hittites, and the Amonites and the Perizites,

who were doomed to destruction because of their sins,
could have been worse than England ! " And again in
the same letter she rather naïvely remarks, a propos of
her enjoyment of the English upper classes :

" For one thing they are far more like *Americans* than
the classes below them. I am quite convinced that we
Americans are in a further state of evolution than the
English. What is rare with them is universal with us. . . .
And they sigh for our special developments of freedom,
and large-heartedness, and unconventionality, and spirit
of progress."

Nevertheless, for all her appreciation of America and
American institutions, she had one desire which America
could not satisfy. When she was a little girl she had read
in her democratic American home a story called *The
Earl's Daughter*, and she did long to move among the blue-
blooded British aristocracy. To stay at Eastnor Castle—
" A genuine Castle, with towers, and turrets, and battle-
ments "—was a real joy ; and to find Lady Henry, as
she thought, so charming, so simple, and so Christian,
was joy in addition. Nor was her visit without influence
on Lady Henry's career. In the whirl of her determined
enthusiasm she induced Lady Henry, first, to stand for the
Presidency of the British Women's Temperance Association, and secondly, to accompany her on a speaking tour
in the United States, after which, she hoped, Lady Henry
would reorganize the British movement on the American
model, and before long there would be an enormous

World Temperance Convention in London, " to which our grand American women will *come in a flood* ! " So, in October 1891, Lady Henry and her new friend set sail, and after ten days of a very rough crossing, which left Lady Henry too limp to talk to " hosts of interviewers, white-ribbon women with flags and bouquets, and a World made of white flowers and a long Adress on Vellum," they landed in New York.

The tour, as a tour, was a great success. Lady Henry was immensely popular, and wherever she went people crowded to hear, see, and touch her—partly, no doubt, because she was an earl's daughter and beautifully dressed, but also because she was so simple and enthusiastic and charming. For her part, she enjoyed the Americans. She found their country beautiful, young, and exciting, " with such a happy, bright, joyous outlook," that, though she disliked what she called the " hopeless vulgarity which prevails," as much as the mosquitoes, the bumpy and ill-made streets and roads, and the hideousness of Chicago, she was easily persuaded to stay over the spring. She met Miss Frances Willard and took to her instantly, while Miss Willard with rather more unrestrained enthusiasm, wrote, " You are my beautiful picture gallery and library, landscape and orchestra. A great hope, a sea to swim in." When such opinions were expressed about her, it was hardly any wonder that Lady Henry wrote to her mother that " your child is spoilt."

However, the spoiling process did not continue when

she got back, with her American laurels thick upon her, to take up her duties as President of the Temperate British Women. It is true that she was an immensely popular president, that the numbers of members greatly increased under her, and that the Association sprang all at once into public notice : this did not endear her to her colleagues. For the British Women, some of whom already thought that Lady Henry possessed " too wide an outlook, too vast an energy, too progressive a mind for our Association," were not at all disposed to receive instructions from the United States as to how their propaganda should be conducted, however much their membership and importance might be enlarged thereby. Nor was it only the American methods to which they objected. If that had been all, one could have had more sympathy with them, for some of the propagandists were distinctly odd fish. There was, for example, the food reform lady who lived largely off a peculiarly repulsive kind of dog-biscuit, which she insisted on pressing upon all and sundry ; and there was the delegate whom hostesses feared to entertain, because when she went to bed she always stripped off the sheets, oiled herself all over, and slept in the blankets. Even the highest in command on the American side had ideas of propaganda which struck others as comic. Miss Willard herself had a pet scheme, called the " Polyglot Petition," which was to draw up an immense petition urging all the rulers of all the countries of the world to raise the standard of their laws to that of Christian principles. This petition, signed by millions of peoples in dozens of languages and stuck on several miles of muslin, was then to be taken in a specially chartered ship all round the world and shown to all the rulers of all the countries. Lady Henry herself thought that the miles of muslin were more likely to move the rulers of the world to amusement than to action ; but in order not to disappoint Miss Willard too cruelly she had a copy of the petition made in two volumes and presented to Queen Victoria, who no doubt received it with interest.

But the main trouble was not over American methods. The main trouble was that Lady Henry, as they had suggested, possessed " too wide an outlook " for the majority of her Executive Committee. Their policy was to preach Total Abstinence from all forms of intoxicating liquor—enforced by law—and nothing else at all. But Lady Henry, as we have seen, could not dissociate in her own mind the drink question from the other social evils which produced it. She had been encouraging branches of the Association to discuss social questions and even women's suffrage, and was rapidly rendering it " impossible for mothers of daughters to bring them to the assemblies," lest their young minds should be corrupted. Worst of all, she was suspected of being shaky on the principle of Total Abstinence. Like other people before her she refused to believe you could not be temperate in the use of alcohol without declining

61

ever to touch it ; and when in 1897 the Royal Commission on the Licensing Laws asked her to give evidence
before it, though she made things very awkward for the
people who profited by the excessive consumption of
strong drink, particularly among the poor, she admitted
that she did not think drinking wrong in itself, and that
she would not wish to make men teetotallers by Act of
Parliament. This, coupled with some correspondence in
the papers which excited a great deal of interest and her
general activities, was sufficient. The Temperate British
Women rushed into battle with most intemperate expres-
sions of their feelings ; and though Lady Henry's popularity with her members in the country was sufficient,
probably, for her to have retained the presidency for as
long as she wished, she had no real heart for continual
internal battles. In 1903 she gave it up, and the Association sank back cheerfully into the sleepy respectability
out of which she had shaken it.

.   .   .   .

The remainder of her life, after a short time spent in
the East End of London, was occupied in work, which,
though unspectacular, was perhaps more deeply satisfactory to her than anything else she had done. In 1895,
some years before, she had founded a colony for convicted
women drunkards at Duxhurst on her Reigate property,
building herself a little cottage from which she could from
time to time supervise the workers in the colony ; and
she now decided to divide her time between this cottage

and a flat in London. It was work for which her earlier troubles, now that hard experience of the world had taught her wisdom, gave her peculiar qualifications. For these women were habitual drunkards, outcasts, that is to say, who were sent to her because there appeared to be no hope of reforming them—and Lady Henry had been an outcast herself, and knew, so well that she could not possibly forget, what it felt like to be an outcast. For this reason she could deal with these unfortunate women as nobody else could ; she never refused admittance to any one, however bad their case, and she never lectured or stormed, but always tried to see " what could be done." As she told a friend, on hearing one woman's story, " I almost felt as though I had done it myself "— and that, no doubt, was the secret of her success. Just as she had been unable, in the Ledbury pubs, and in the Embankment shelters, to condemn without understanding the miserable people she found there, so at Duxhurst she brought many an unfortunate " sinful girl "—for as time went on, and her success began to tell, women were sent her for other crimes than drink—back to life and hope by understanding, without censoriousness, what she had done and why she had done it. At Duxhurst, in fact, as nowhere else, these women were treated not as criminals or persons in need of punishment, but as patients who wanted kindly and sympathetic care—and this before modern theories of " remedial treatment " had gained any general support.

Duxhurst endured until the outbreak of the war, when it became a soldiers' hospital for some time, afterwards returning to its proper use. But in 1921, after only two days' illness, Lady Henry died. One of the later entries in her diary runs, " I wonder if any one can understand how really mediocre I *know* myself to be."

EDITH CAVELL

III

EDITH CAVELL

WHILE the name of Edith Cavell is certainly known
to all in this country, whether or not they read this
book, better than that of any other of its heroines, most
of those who know it would be hard put to it to recall
any facts about her life than its close, in October 1915,
at the hands of a German firing-party in Brussels. Nor
is this surprising, for in truth there is not a great deal
to be known. Edith Cavell's life is not unlike the statue
of her that stands in St. Martin's Place—stiff, austere,
and slightly without expression, as are her photographs.
Of course, the nurse's uniform which she wore tends to
heighten the impression of austerity ; we do not expect
people who are at the head of a nursing institute to be
very skittish or very undecided, or even very prone to
chatter. Nevertheless, in Edith Cavell's case it was more
than the uniform. She was rigidly brought up ; she had,
from very early years, a vocation to which she firmly
and rigidly adhered ; she was, in fact, the type of cool,

rather stiff, devoted personality which so exactly represents one part of English life. And she was uncommunicative about herself and her opinions. Even that oft-quoted remark which is inscribed upon her statue, " *Patriotism is not enough,*" is enigmatic. Nobody knows exactly what Nurse Cavell meant to convey by it.

She was born in 1865, the elder of the two daughters of the Reverend Frederick Cavell, incumbent of Swardeston, a small village near Norwich, where he inhabited the New Rectory, so called not because it was in any way new, but to distinguish it from the Old Rectory which was in ruins. Frederick Cavell did not live to see his daughter grow up, but long enough to educate her in the stiff principles of an English rectory in the mid-nineteenth century. He appears to have been something of a holy terror in the village, whose souls he looked after for more than forty years before he died. He preached to them on Sundays sermons not of a cheerful, breezy type, but stern exhortations to live in obedience to the dictates of duty ; and if any parishioner, particularly any well-off or pretentious parishioner, appeared to him to have failed in the pursuit of his duty, he did not hesitate to haul him over the coals in public, either in church on the Sunday or in one of the general gatherings—almost like a Parish Council before Parish Councils were invented—which were regularly held in the big rectory garden by the churchyard. One of the very few personal reminiscences which we have of Edith Cavell's childhood is her recollection of the mulberry tree in the rectory garden, from whose produce her mother used to make that peculiarly unpleasant concoction, mulberry jam ; the other is of the Cavell régime on a Sunday—no books, no games, no needlework ; catechism first, then two church services, and devotional reading aloud in the evenings. Uncommon, and rather formidable to think of in these days, but not at all unusual in those.

Apart from that we know really very little about her, save that she was a cheerful, good-looking, dark-haired child, and that, like Florence Nightingale, she showed quite early a passion for sick nursing. When she was only nine years old she was missed one evening and did not return all night. When she was found, it was at the house of a sick neighbour whom she had gone to see, and had found in the throes of a sudden attack and with no one to look after her. Like a born nurse she stayed with her, not thinking to let anybody know until help arrived. (In after years, when people asked her why she had become a nurse, she answered with surprise, " Why, how could I have been anything else ? ")

On the death of Edith's father, her mother moved to a house in Norwich, and Edith was sent to school in Brussels. Nothing whatever is known of her schooldays ; as in after years she started her hospital in Brussels, it may be conjectured that she did not dislike the city, but the only other thing which can be said is that her Belgian training was the beginning of what is still quite rare, even among the heads of the nursing profession—a long and varied acquaintance with foreign countries.

The details of her career, up till the year 1906, can be very quickly told. She always knew she would have to earn her living, for the emoluments, then as now, of the majority of country clergymen did not suffice to provide their children with independent incomes ; and she had always intended to earn it as a nurse. But the profession of nursing, which to-day is badly enough paid, was then even less remunerative, so that it was fortunate for her that, when she was twenty-two, a relative died and left her a legacy which enabled her to pursue her training in other ways than by the dismal road of being a ward-nurse—*i.e.* a kind of general servant—and then a probationer in a large hospital. Her nephew, her sister's son, of whom she was very fond, has left it on record that the legacy was large enough to have enabled her, had she chosen, to live modestly upon it without working ; but she preferred to stick to her job, and expend the money upon making herself a more efficient nurse.

She went first to study in Switzerland, and then to Bavaria, where she gave her services voluntarily to a hospital run by a Dr. Wolfenburg. Dr. Wolfenburg would seem to have been a boorish kind of man ; for, though Edith Cavell, finding that his hospital was seriously lacking in certain vital types of apparatus, provided it out of her own pocket, he showed no gratitude, holding that contributions ought to be made direct to the hospital funds, and not earmarked for specific purposes. Nevertheless, Edith enjoyed her stay in Germany. She thought highly of German methods, and became sincerely attached to the people—a fact not without importance for her later life.

In 1896, being then twenty-nine years old, she entered herself as a nurse at the London Hospital, and within a year was put upon the staff, where she remained for five years. Two years after her appointment there was a general outbreak of typhoid fever in Maidstone, which became so serious that the local authorities were unable to cope with it. They appealed for assistance, and the London Hospital sent down a team in the charge of Edith Cavell. It was her first experience of running a hospital on her own, even though the hospital staff only consisted of herself and six other nurses. It appears that she did her job competently, and that her work at the London Hospital was appreciated. After six years of it, however, she turned to gain experience in poor law nursing, and served in the poor law infirmaries of Shoreditch and Highgate. While there she made the acquaintance of a lady called Miss Stone, who became one of her few intimate friends, and to whom we are indebted for the little we have in the way of personal impressions of her. But she found the work hard—poor law work, among the most wretched classes of the population, does tend to be very hard and hopeless—and she was forced to take a rest, which she spent travelling in Switzerland

and Italy. (As almost the only " hobby " which she possessed was a taste for painting, it may be conjectured that she enjoyed a holiday among the Italian art galleries.) On her return to England she took temporary charge of a Queen's District Nursery in Manchester, but shortly afterwards was approached by Dr. Depage, head of a Belgian military hospital, to assist him in the establishment of better training for Belgian nurses, and in 1906 she left England for Brussels. She never returned to live in her own country.

Her work in Brussels met with immediate and recognized success. Within a year of her arrival there Dr. Depage had appointed her the first matron of his clinic, the Berkendael Medical Institute, which rapidly became a national establishment of considerable importance. Just before the war the Belgian Government officially recognized this institute, and devoted state funds to providing it with a new and larger building. At the same time, Edith Cavell was also organizing and managing another hospital in Brussels, the hospital of St. Gilles, and running a training school for nurses, as well as becoming an international authority on nursing problems— she attended and spoke at International Nursing Congresses in London. So well was she known, and so popular in Brussels was her institute and her work, that when in 1914 the German armies invaded and conquered Belgium, the military authorities gave her permission to remain and to turn the Institute Berkendael

NURSE CAVELL.

into a Red Cross Hospital for the wounded of all nationalities. (Dr. Depage had by this time departed to organize military hospitals at the front.)

Miss Cavell's success was partly due to her having introduced a new standard of work and education into the Belgian tradition of nursing. Prior to her arrival in Brussels, the majority of the nurses obtainable in Belgium had been nuns, members of one or another of the Roman Catholic communities in Belgium. No doubt the nuns were very devoted, but their training and education were not such as to give them much knowledge of the principles of modern hygiene, which are of the first importance in caring for sick persons. They were poor, not always too clean, and their clothes—not such a trivial matter as it sounds—were highly unsuitable for wearing in a hospital. Miss Cavell herself pointed out, in some articles that she wrote for a paper called the *Nursing Mirror*, that the contrast between the sombre, heavy wrappings and veilings of the nuns and their nursing sisters, and the clean blue linen frocks, white aprons and sleeves, and " Sister Dora " bonnets of her own nurses, served as a kind of symbol of the difference between the old order and the new ; but it was the type of nurse as well as the type of uniform that she strove to change. Hitherto, nursing in Belgium had not only been confined to the Catholic sisterhood, thereby cutting out the very large number of Belgian Protestants ; it had also been accepted as a profession which only nuns or very poor women could enter.

Now, not every girl who wants to be a nurse also wants to be a nun ; and Miss Cavell, by taking and giving training to novices of all classes, rapidly built up a staff of nurses, English, Belgian, and German, which provided an example to the world of what the profession might be like. The growth of the numbers who were working under her, from a tiny handful in 1906 to nearly a hundred by 1914, shows how the work was prospering.

At this point we may perhaps try to discover something about the character of Edith Cavell ; but it is not too easy. It is always unfortunate for the biographer, when his subject, after a life spent in the quiet and comparative undistinguished pursuit of her chosen career, dies suddenly in a blaze of martyrdom. For when people become martyrs nothing but what is extravagantly, even ridiculously laudable, can be said of them ; and all the memoirs and biographies of Edith Cavell were published immediately after her death, when it would have been almost treason to say that she was anything but a saint with no human weaknesses whatever. When one reads, in an eloquent life of her by a Frenchman, that people called her " the angel from England," and that her patients thought she was something sent down from heaven, one can only sigh and wish for some rather more helpful information.

Her friend Miss Stone has told us as much as anybody else, and that is not very much ; for Miss Stone, however much she loved her, clearly stood rather in awe of Miss

Cavell. We are told that " she was one of the noblest women who ever lived," that she was extraordinarily courageous and self-controlled, and that, though her health was not particularly robust, she never gave in until she could no longer stand on her feet, unless expressly ordered to rest by a doctor. But we are also told that the first impression of her was of a woman very kind at heart, but stern and unbending in manner ; that she had a rigidly high standard of work which she enforced both on herself and on those who served under her ; that no detail was beneath her strict consideration, and that the one type of worker whom she could not endure was the one who was half-hearted about her work—" though she had a real sense of humour, she would never tolerate anything like a joke among her subordinates when they were on duty." Also, she was extremely reserved ; she hardly ever spoke, even to Miss Stone, of her intimate thoughts, and whatever affection she may have had for her friend, she expressed it in action and never at all in words.

Altogether, it would seem from this picture rather a formidable personality, and one of which the novices who worked under her may well have been in awe. Nevertheless, the absolute justice of her mind, and the real understanding of different temperaments which she possessed, seem to have triumphed over these obstacles and to have caused everybody with whom she came in contact to regard her with deep respect and affection.

Perhaps the best summary of her life and character at this point was uttered by herself—one of her rare recorded remarks—in conversation with a friend. " In most people's eyes," she said, " I am only a lonely old maid " (she was then forty-eight), " but I have my mother to care for, I have my work which I love, and so I am such a happy old maid that everybody would envy me if they knew how happy I am." Not a bad summary on the whole.

.   .   .   .

When the European War broke out Edith Cavell was in England, paying a visit to her mother in Norwich. She was not due in Brussels until September ; but as soon as she heard the news she hurried back to her post, where her first duty was to arrange for the repatriation of the German patients in her institute to their own country. By the time that this was done the city of Brussels had resigned itself to wait for the invasion. As everybody who has read the history of the war knows, the march of the German armies was held up at first for a few days by the resistance put up by the Belgian frontier fortresses of Liège and Namur ; and there were some Belgians who hoped that this delay would give time for the French army and the British Expeditionary Force to relieve Brussels, but they were disappointed. On 20th August the Germans marched in, and Brussels was a German town until November 1918.

The invasion of Belgium was, of course, one of the

acts of the German Empire which roused British public opinion most solidly against it ; and later on, when war propaganda was at its height, " Belgian atrocities " (many of them invented for the purpose) were published in the newspapers of the Allies in order to whip up anti-German feeling. But, as a measure of how far war has " progressed " since 1914, it is interesting to see that the actual occupation of Brussels took place with little violence and even with comparatively little ill-feeling on either side. No Press campaign proving that the Belgians were uncivilized outcasts had preceded it ; no 'planes spraying gas-bombs and liquid fire had heralded the German approach. All that happened was that rumours spread steadily that the Belgian army was broken and the Germans approaching ; then there was a sound of trumpets at the gates ; the civil guard laid down its arms and opened them ; and a number of weary and footsore soldiers marched into the town, many of them unaware where they were and thinking it was Paris they had reached, and more quite at a loss to know, if Brussels it really was, what on earth they were supposed to be doing in Brussels. Miss Cavell, who no less than any one else regarded the occupation of Belgium as a crime, was quite as much concerned with the exhaustion and unhappiness of the German soldiers torn from their families and flinging themselves down, too tired to eat, on the stones of the Brussels streets ; and she described, in an article subsequently published in the *Nursing*

Mirror, how the citizens of Brussels chatted in German (those of them who could speak it) with their invaders, and how the German soldiers fed the Belgian children on chocolate, and gave them rides on their horses. Not so was the 1936 invasion of a capital city conducted.

It was in this sort of spirit that Edith Cavell was given leave, by the German occupying authorities, to continue to conduct her hospital under Red Cross auspices, as a general hospital for the wounded of all nationalities. But before long she found that, even in 1914, matters could not very long proceed on this comparatively friendly basis. The first hint of a clash came with a suggestion that hospitals should be responsible for seeing that enemy—*i.e.* anti-German—prisoners did not escape from them. This Miss Cavell haughtily refused to do : she was conducting a hospital, she explained, not a jail, and for the moment this explanation seemed to pass muster. But there were more difficulties to come.

Those who remember, or who have read the story of the events of August and September 1914, will know with what a swift and alarming sweep the northern wing of the German armies, after the brief check at the frontier, marched right across Belgium and northern France, only to be stayed, when they were all but within striking distance of Paris, by the fierce fighting on the Marne. In such an attack it was inevitable that a great number of French, and later of English soldiers, should be left behind in the wake of the conquering armies ; and that the " occupied territory "—occupied, of course by the Germans—should contain many " enemy " soldiers, some of whom were wounded, more or less severely, but others of whom had not even fired a shot, because the German troops had simply swept by, leaving them in the rear. Large numbers of these men, not prisoners of war, because they had not been captured, but simply fugitive soldiers in country that was now nominally German, drifted back into Brussels and adjoining towns, and there they presented a problem. In so far as they were wounded they received attention, along with the German wounded, in the Red Cross hospitals ; and Miss Cavell, as we have already seen, made it quite clear that she would not under any circumstances act as a jailer to her patients—*i.e.* that if they wanted to escape into Holland, which was a neutral country, and could manage it, she would not interfere with them. But there were the others, those who were not wounded, but who wanted to get back to their own countries, and probably, in the case of those who were of military age, to return and fight the Germans. At some time during the early months of the war— exactly when it has never been quite clear—these men began to come to Miss Cavell for assistance in getting across the frontier. And she helped them.

It should be made quite clear that Miss Cavell knew perfectly well what she was doing, and that she was doing it at her own risk, though she may not have fully realized that the risk she was running was the risk of death. Von

Bissing, who after the occupation of Brussels had been made governor of the whole of Belgium, was well aware of the possibility of a leakage of able-bodied enemies back to their own countries, and in a proclamation issued quite early in his tenure of office he made it plain that it was an offence which would be severely punished to assist any such " enemy " to escape from Belgium. Nevertheless, Edith Cavell continued her work, and there is no doubt, from letters which she admitted to having received, that she did assist to escape persons who afterwards fought against Germany.

Even so, it was some time before any action was taken against her. She was immensely popular in Brussels, and her policy of succouring wounded Germans equally with her own countrymen—continuing to do her job, in fact, without asking any questions about the nationality of those she helped—made the German authorities very careful about taking action against her until they had plenty of evidence. But when they did strike, they struck hard and suddenly. According to one story they made use of spies, who took a secretary of Miss Cavell's out to tea, and under pretence of being English soldiers trying to escape, got her to describe to them in detail all that Miss Cavell was doing to help the English and the French. But it is not necessary either to believe or disbelieve that story : the point is that Miss Cavell was knowingly disobeying the commands of the German rulers of Belgium, and the only question was when and

by what means her activities would be stopped. On the
morning of the 5th August 1915 a corporal with five
soldiers called to arrest Miss Cavell. She was taken to a
cell in the prison of St. Gilles, from which she was never
again released.

It was some time before any one in England knew
what had happened ; and when they did there was little
enough that they could do. Naturally, as the whole of
Belgium was now in German hands, there was no English
diplomatic representative available there. Sir Edward
Grey, who was then Foreign Secretary, immediately
upon receipt of the news got into communication with
the United States representative, Mr. Brand Whitlock,
and asked him to do all he could to ensure Miss Cavell's
safety. (For the first two and a half years of the war,
before the United States became a belligerent, American
diplomatists were continually being called upon to act
as mediators between the warring countries.)

Mr. Whitlock, who was startled and shocked by the
arrest, did all he could to help ; but his first letters
elicited no reply from the German authorities. Later he
was informed that the prisoner had confessed her guilt,
and that a defender would be provided for her at her
court-martial. After some chopping and changing, her
defence was in fact handed over to M. Sadi Kirschner,
a lawyer, member of the Brussels Bar, who, as a Belgian,
no doubt did all he could under the circumstances.

But the circumstances were peculiarly difficult for

him. Not that any special procedure was adopted in Edith Cavell's case ; it was before the days when dictatorships invented new laws and new forms of law to suit their convenience or their idea of what was for the public benefit. Edith Cavell was to be tried according to German military law, as a spy ; but that law did not allow her defender to see her or talk to her before the court-martial, nor was he even permitted, as the defence in any ordinary criminal or civil case is permitted, to see the evidence— *i.e.* the documents, depositions of spies, statements of the prisoners, herself, etc.—on which the prosecution was basing its case. So on the day of the court-martial, 7th October 1915, M. Kirschner entered upon his task practically in the dark, being unaware of what the outside evidence was against her, or what admissions she had made to her accusers when she had no advocate to advise her what she should say.

When he arrived at the court-martial he found that his task was all but hopeless. Edith Cavell was arraigned, with thirty-five other persons, on the charge of having facilitated the escape of enemy subjects from Belgium into neutral territory. This was, naturally, an offence against German military law ; but it was not a capital offence. However, the prosecution further asserted, and was prepared to prove, on Miss Cavell's own confession, that she had actually assisted Belgians of military age to return to the battle-front, and that she had provided English and French soldiers with funds and with guides

82

to enable them to get across the frontier and so back to their own countries—in order, presumably, to fight once more against the Germans. It was also said that she herself had admitted to having received letters from repatriated soldiers, thanking her for enabling them to " fight another day." If that were so, the German prosecutor contended, she was clearly guilty of attempts to conduct soldiers back to the enemy fronts ; and for that, under the German military code, the penalty was death.

We do not know, nor shall we ever know, how much truth there was in all this, whether in fact Edith Cavell ever made any such statement. But that she did is at least highly probable. She had certainly been assisting French, English, and Belgian soldiers to escape, and it is highly unlikely—indeed, on what is known of her character, almost impossible—that she restricted her services to those who were not possible soldiers. She had already said that her hospital was not a prison. Of course, if she had been a prisoner awaiting trial under peace-time codes, she would have been in communication with her lawyer, who would have advised her to admit nothing, but to leave to the other side the burden of proving anything which they wanted to prove. But she was alone, and not conversant with the law. She had been nine weeks in prison, and what we know of her suggests that she possessed the kind of simple honesty which admits its actions without considering the consequences.

However that may be, by the time that M. Kirschner was called upon to aid his client, the question of her guilt was already an accomplished fact. The court-martial ended on 8th October, with the decision that Edith Cavell was guilty of espionage, for which the penalty was death. The only question remaining was whether the sentence would be carried out. Mr. Whitlock was in hope that it would not be. It was many years since the " civilized " countries had put a woman to death for spying, and he thought that the German Government would not care to set a new precedent. He was wrong. On the evening of 11th October he was informed that sentence of death had been pronounced and would be carried out the following morning. His last-minute efforts, strenuous as they were, were unavailing, and at 2 a.m. on the morning of 12th October Edith Cavell was shot by a firing-party. The story told afterwards by a journalist named Harden, that the soldiers refused to finish her off, so that an officer had to fulfil that duty, was not confirmed, and can be regarded as war-time propaganda. She had been found guilty of espionage, and she was to pay the penalty.

The utmost concession that Mr. Whitlock could achieve was that the English chaplain of Christ Church in Brussels should be allowed to visit Miss Cavell before her death. To him, therefore, we are indebted for the report of what she wished conveyed to the world on the eve of her death. "I am not afraid or apprehensive," she said. "I have seen death so often" (and what nurse, particularly in war-time, has not?) "that it does not seem to me strange or terrible. I thank God for these ten weeks of rest before the end. Life has always been troubled and full of problems ; this time of rest has been very welcome. Every one about me has been very good to me, but I want to say, now that I face God and eternity, that I realize that patriotism is not enough. I must not hate or feel bitter towards anybody."

The news of Edith Cavell's execution created an immense storm in the Press of all the Allied countries. Of course, as is to be expected during war-time, the utmost was made of any incident that could be used as anti-German propaganda ; and the hysterical articles which appeared in the English and French newspapers declared that Nurse Cavell was a martyr, a saint without flaw, and that the country responsible for her death could only be composed of human monsters. Some of these statements Nurse Cavell herself would have been the first to repudiate ; but it cannot be denied that public opinion, even apart from the Press, was very strongly moved. The memorial service in St. Paul's was thronged, and— perhaps a more important sign of feeling—for some days after the news became known the recruiting stations in England were crowded with men anxious to enlist to avenge her. As recruiting propaganda, the death of Edith Cavell was a gift to Great Britain, and probably brought many more men into the army than she had assisted to return from Belgium—though, of course, the idea that it turned the tide of the war is ludicrous. The war went on long after the thought of " avenging Edith Cavell " had ceased to inspire anybody to volunteer. But it was in relation to its immediate effects that her execution was described as " not merely a crime, but a blunder "—it was by no means the only blunder made by the German High Command.

As to whether it was or was not a crime, opinions have differed and will probably continue to differ. The German Government did not defend itself beyond saying officially that Edith Cavell had been found guilty, largely on her own confession, of an offence for which the German military law prescribed the death penalty. This was admittedly so : on the other hand, nobody suggests that she was guilty of what people commonly mean when they talk about " spying." She had not striven to find out military secrets or disclose them to the enemy ; she had done, in fact, nothing of which any ordinary person could have under any circumstances have been ashamed. Nor, however, has a soldier who dies in battle ; Edith Cavell in effect died in battle, and the main reason for the rush of public feeling was that it outraged British sentiment that a woman should be put to death, whatever offences she had committed against military law. In fact, British military tribunals did not sentence women spies to death ; but presumably the German High Command, with less sensitiveness, decided that the bad propaganda effect of Miss Cavell's death was less of a danger than the continued existence in Brussels of a pro-Ally centre for escaping prisoners.

At that we may leave it, merely noting that now, nineteen years after the Armistice, the fury of national hatred which was born in the war and the peace treaties has grown to such a pitch that the death of half a dozen Edith Cavells, with or without trial, would probably make no more than a passing paragraph in the newspapers. Those last words of Edith Cavell's, *Patriotism is not enough*, are incised upon the base of her statue by Trafalgar Square : it would have been better if they had been written on the minds of the statesmen who dictated the Treaty of Versailles.

MARY MACARTHUR

MARY MACARTHUR

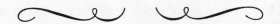

IN days past, when distinguished old gentlemen who were not distinguished for their ability to make speeches were asked to preside at school prize-givings, they used quite frequently to annoy the masters or mistresses who had to listen to them by proclaiming that it signified very little whether or not a boy or girl won prizes or commendation at school, that they themselves had always been the naughtiest (or the stupidest) boy in their class, and it had not mattered at all to them, etc. etc. That type of remark is now rather less common ; people are less inclined to be proud of being dunces, or thrashed so many times a term ; and few now hold that the most unsatisfactory schoolboy is likely to turn out the most satisfactory man. Indeed, if it was ever true of boys, it was certainly not true of girls, as a reading of the other chapters of this book will show.

But, all the same, it does sometimes happen that a school child who is no credit to her school turns out to possess qualities which, unappreciated by the authorities, are exactly those which are required to make her a success in her life's work ; and, in such a case, it all depends on whether the girl in question can find her life's work, or have it shown to her, before it is too late. Mary Macarthur, the organizer of underpaid women's labour, who became far and away the most powerful personality among Labour women, and who died in 1921, barely forty years old, and with her life's work only half done, was such a girl ; and it was fortunate for her that by the time she was twenty-three the cause to which she was to devote herself so abundantly had been already made plain. Thereafter, the very qualities which had militated against her in school, her enthusiasm, her waves of temperament and passion, her carelessness of anything that she was supposed to know or supposed to do, compared with what she had set her heart on, became assets in making her one of the most brilliant organizers and negotiators the Labour Movement has ever possessed.

She was born in Glasgow in 1880. Her father's people came from the Highlands and her mother's from Aberdeen, and it may be conjectured that this inheritance of the fire and romance of the Celt, combined with the solid sense of reality which is supposed to be the peculiar possession of the Scot from the plains, gave her exactly the qualities which she needed for success.

Success, however, was not " apparent from the first," as it seems to be with some people. At twelve years old she was sent to Glasgow High School, where she remained for three years ; but, as related, the period of her schooldays was stormy and of little result. She had ability ; once she won a medal for the best work of the year, and she wrote essays and anything which entered her head with fervour, but without much discrimination. Even in later years, though her journalistic style was always vigorous, her literary judgment was almost *nil*, and she was always liable to disconcert her admirers by quoting, in her most impassioned speeches, long passages of verse which she herself found extremely moving, but which her hearers considered unmitigated doggerel. For the rest she was a child of violent emotions, often confided to her diary, and generally lasting for a very little while. A teacher who could stimulate her to the naïve resolve, " My nails *shall* be beautiful," turns out to be after all " not the ideal woman I have imagined "; and other adorations follow the same course—much as, when she was a married woman with a home of her own, she was always telling her friends that she had engaged a perfect paragon of a maid, only to discover, a few weeks or months later, that the perfect paragon drank, or stole, or had other equally undesirable traits. She was quite conscious of, and sometimes in despair about, her own shortcomings. " I *will* change my character," one entry in her diary reads. " I will be cold, calm, unemotional." Fortunately for herself and for us, this ambition was not fulfilled ; but another—" I must, I will be famous "—came more true.

After her schooldays were ended she tossed about—there is no other phrase which really expresses it—for some time uneasily. She was sent to Germany for a year ; she returned to Ayr, whither her father had removed his business in 1895 ; for some time she seemed in ill-health. Really she was profoundly bored. There was, or seemed, nothing whatever for her to do ; she was not prepared to sit down at home and wait for somebody to marry her ; she had not been trained for any particular job ; and doing some work for the local Primrose League and writing a few articles for the local papers was not nearly enough to absorb her superabundant energies. In desperation she persuaded her father to take her into his business as a book-keeper ; and thus, though she did not know it at the time, her future life was settled.

Mr. Macarthur's business was a well-established drapery store, with what is commonly known as " excellent connections." He was a considerable and respected citizen, Conservative in politics and a pillar of the Primrose League, though his general outlook was certainly on the Liberal side, and he was both proud and fond of his elder daughter. It certainly did not seem as though entry into this business was likely to turn Mary Macarthur into an eager and passionate Socialist.

But it made the start, by bringing her into contact with her father's employees and workers in the shop as well as with the more respectable clerks and bookkeepers ; she became quickly popular among them—as indeed, she did almost wherever she went—and, as Scotland is and has always been a much less snobbish country than England, she mixed with them much more than might have been the case had she been living farther south. So it happened that, when in 1901 one John Turner appeared in Ayr, in order to try and found there a branch of the National Amalgamated Union of Shop Assistants, Warehousemen, and Clerks, the local Conservative newspaper, wishing to print a contemptuous article about the absurdity of Trade Unionism, and remembering Mary Macarthur as a promising writer, commissioned her to go to his meeting and write them a column, " preferably of a facetious character," about it. She accepted the commission, and duly went to the meeting ; but she never wrote her column for the Conservative paper.

Nowadays Trade Unionism is a perfectly recognized and respectable thing. When the Trades Union Congress meets, all the newspapers print reports of its debates, and the A.A. puts up large yellow notices telling motorists who wish to attend it which way they should go. Many employers prefer that their workmen should be members of a Trade Union which can discuss wages and hours for the trade as a whole, and only a few extreme Conservatives wish that there were no Trade Unions at all. But thirty-five years ago this was not so. There was no Labour Party ; there were many who thought (in spite of the writings of Mr. and Mrs. Sidney Webb) that Trade Unions were the invention of the devil, and that, even if dirty and rowdy miners and factory workers joined Unions, would-be respectable clerks and shop assistants should not have anything to do with them. In 1901 John Turner, who was for many years General Secretary of the Shop Assistants' Union and a member of the General Council of the Trades Union Congress, had much ado to get shop assistants even to come to a meeting in Ayr.

He tried, however, and he succeeded in getting together " a fairly well-attended meeting in a dark and dreary schoolhouse in an obscure part of the town."

" Among those present," he wrote long afterwards, " I noticed an animated group of young ladies in the centre of the room, with a laughing, vivacious, fair-haired girl in their midst." The " young ladies " were the employees of Mr. Macarthur ; the " fair-haired girl " was Mary.

All public speakers who are any good at their jobs learn to do one thing, to pick out the important members of their audience, to discover, by looking at the faces, who it is that they must aim at convincing. John Turner picked out Mary Macarthur, and he directed his arguments to convincing her. He spoke of the history of Trade Unionism, of what these small bands of workers, paying their contributions of a few pence a week out of their meagre earnings, had been able to do for their fellows. He told of the wages that had been raised, of the hours of work that had been reduced, and of the working conditions that had been improved through joint action ; and he showed how the better employers, in many trades, preferred that there should be a Union which would stand up for the rights of the workers, and would help them to bring up the wages paid by the bad firms, and so prevent their competing unfairly with those who were willing to pay decent rates. Finally, when he had finished his speech and answered all the questions which the meeting put to him, he asked her point-blank whether she would join the Shop Assistants' Union. She hesitated ; she doubted whether, as the daughter of the proprietor, she was eligible to join a Union meant for his employees. But her conversion was complete from that moment. Even at the meeting she told him that she thought that all her father's employees ought to join ; and shortly afterwards, at his earnest request, she agreed to become the first chairman of the Ayr branch of the Shop Assistants' Union. She had found her job.

Once she had found it she went ahead rapidly. There was plenty of work to be done, for the lot of shop assistants at the beginning of the century was often very hard indeed. There was no early closing day then ; the law limited the hours which might be worked by employees in factories, but said nothing about shop assistants, and it was perfectly possible for children of twelve and thirteen to be worked from early morning till late at night. Furthermore, wages were very low, and a good many shop assistants " lived in "—that is to say, in rooms or barracks provided by their employer, in which they had to submit to his rules and eat what food he chose to give them. An employer who was inhuman and unimaginative, therefore, could turn service in a shop into virtual slavery and semi-starvation, and the law did not protect his assistants (unless he used actual violence on them) in any way. The Factory Acts, which after the long struggles of the nineteenth century had been passed to protect the factory worker, to a certain extent, from overwork and ill-treatment, did not apply to shops. (Nor do they now, though a certain amount of separate legislation has been passed in the interest of shop and office workers.)

The Shop Assistants' Union was small and struggling. But it had enlisted the interest of influential and enlightened people who were struggling to get better conditions for the working classes, and Mary Macarthur quickly came into contact with people who were trying to change the law and to make a better social system. She met Sir Charles Dilke and his wife, who devoted most of their lives to a long crusade on behalf of the " bottom dog " ; and she also met the pioneers of Socialism in Scotland, such as Robert Smillie, long the leader of the Miners' Federation, and Keir Hardie, the founder of the Labour Party. When she went to John Turner's meeting it is doubtful whether she had even heard of Socialism, but within a year or two she was a convinced Socialist. Like many others of her generation, it was only necessary that she should know that a faith called Socialism existed for her to embrace it with all the fervour that she had previously bestowed upon schoolgirl adorations—but this adoration was to last.

Meantime her vivid personality and her organizing gifts rapidly made her an important person in her Union. She became the president of its Scottish section ; she represented Scotland at the Union's annual conferences ; in 1903, only two years after the meeting at Ayr, she was a member of its Executive Committee, speaking and acting in equality with Margaret Bondfield (later to become the first woman Cabinet Minister), and with men more than twice her age. Fortunately for her, the Shop Assistants' Union, being a comparatively new organization, was not obsessed by the prejudice against women which long disfigured some of the older Unions * ; talent, in whatever sex it made its appearance, was readily recognized, and hers was recognized with great rapidity. She was only twenty-three.

But it was not long before she began to feel that she could not stay in Scotland. It was partly because her

---

* There were Unions which refused membership to women ; others which took their subscriptions and denied them votes. One granted them votes, but provided that the vote of one man should be equal to those of twenty-five women !

new avocations were bound to bring her more and more into disagreement with her family. Mr. Macarthur, as a broad-minded man, could see that there was a case for Trade Unionists, but for Socialism he could not see that there was any case at all ; it seemed to him an invention of the devil and peculiarly abominable in women. Mary was far too fond of her family to wish to quarrel with them ; besides, the position of any public worker who is preaching, in her own town, doctrines which her family abominates is always bound to be very unpleasant. But, even more than that, she was anxious to try her wings in a wider field than Scotland. In 1903, therefore, she took her courage in both hands and travelled to London. She had not secured a job beforehand ; but she was confident that she would get one, and, in fact, she almost immediately found a post as book-keeper in Brixton. She was not, however, allowed to retain it, for Margaret Bondfield insisted that she should apply for the post of secretary to the Women's Trade Union League.

At that time the Women's Trade Union League had already been in existence for some time. It had been founded in 1874, and its purpose was to secure better wages and conditions for women by getting them to organize together. Wages for women workers in almost all industries were shockingly low. What they were in 1903 is unknown ; but a little later, in 1906, a Royal Commission discovered that their highest average earnings (in the textile trades) were 15s. 5d. a week, and that, taking the yearly earnings of the women workers of Great Britain as a whole, the average per week was only 10s. 10½d.—this at a time when the average for men was 25s. 9d. And even from these wages there were often deductions, to pay for the thread used by tailoresses, and so on.

There were many reasons to account for this. To some extent it was due to the fact that women did not serve the long apprenticeships and gain the same skill that men did in certain trades. Even more, it was because a good many of those who were working were girls or young women who were either not supporting themselves entirely (because they lived at home), or who were looking forward to marrying and being supported by some man, and so did not much care what they earned, so long as they earned something ; or they were widows whom the death of their husbands had forced to go out to work in order to get food for the children, and who had to take whatever job turned up, no matter how badly paid it was. And, beyond this, there was a sort of ill-defined tradition, in everywhere except the Lancashire cotton trade, where piece-work * rates were equal, that women's work was less good than men's, and should be paid less—though it is difficult to imagine that any one

* " Piece-work " means being paid according to the amount of work done. " Time-work " means being paid so much a week or day or hour.

seriously believed that a woman's work was less than half as good as a man's.

Whatever the reasons the result was most unfortunate. For there were, as there always have been, a great number of women working who were not living at home or partly supported by somebody else, and these women had to try and eke out an existence—and sometimes bring up children—on the miserable wages mentioned above. Furthermore, where it was possible for a woman to do the work that a man had been doing, there was a perpetual temptation to mean and unscrupulous firms—or even firms that were simply in difficulties—to dismiss their male employees and substitute women at less than half the cost ; and the sight of men, who were perhaps fathers of families, turned out of work which was given to girls was not likely to make a happy situation. (It must be remembered that at that time there was no unemployment benefit for those thrown out of work. If a man had saved something out of his wages—not too easy if he had a family of young children—he could live for a while on that. If he was a member of a Trade Union which had a high subscription and an unemployment fund—which meant that he must have been earning good enough wages to pay a fairly high weekly sum to his Union—he would get help for a little while. Apart from that, he would have to go to the Poor Law, or beg for charity, or starve.)

The only way, really, to deal with this problem of

shockingly low wages for women was to organize them into Trade Unions, so that they could go to the employers in a body and ask to have their wages raised. As Mary Macarthur pointed out again and again, if a single worker asks for a rise there is a simple way to deal with her—dismiss her. Another can easily be found to take her place ; whereas if all the workers in a factory or shop simultaneously ask for a rise it is not nearly so easy. But organizing the women was a difficult job. Those who were only using their earnings as pocket-money did not care, and would not be bothered ; and the others, particularly the widows with children, were too afraid of being sacked, of losing the miserable amount which they could earn, to ask for any more. Nor were the men's Unions, which were much stronger, always helpful. They were afraid of the women getting their jobs at lower rates ; and they often tried simply to keep the women out, instead of raising their wages so that they would not be able to undercut them. In later years Mary Macarthur received an appeal which she often quoted as showing how, gradually, the men came to see that this attitude was short-sighted. It ran as follows : " Will you please send an organizer at once to a town where wages are very low, for our Amalgamated Society has decided that if the women of this town cannot be organized they must be exterminated." This was not perhaps the most elegant way of putting it, but it shows the need there was for a Women's Trade Union League.

Not all of the men's Unions were as short-sighted as this. In the Lancashire cotton industry, where women had always worked alongside men, the Trade Unions had steadily supported the Women's Trade Union League. So also, though with less vigour because its membership was less, had Mary Macarthur's own Union, the Shop Assistants ; and others of the men's Unions had gradually joined up. Nevertheless, when Mary took over the secretaryship the League was not in a good way. It was continually trying to found Trade Unions for women, which mostly petered out owing either to lack of interest or to fear on the part of the women whom it was trying to organize. As Mrs. Hamilton in her life of Mary Macarthur puts it, " The task appeared to be that of a man seeking to strike foundations in a swamp. With great difficulty a pile is driven in—only to be sucked down and covered up again." And if there were no organizations the women's wages could not be raised, and the keen ones who had joined would lose heart, wonder what they were getting for the subscription that caused them so much self-sacrifice to pay, and drop out. " Your new secretary," said Lady Dilke, the chairman, " must be an organizer who can *rouse* them."

From the moment at which she took over her new office Mary Macarthur performed this function most effectively. Indeed, throughout her life her mission seemed to be to rouse people ; and if occasionally she aroused others besides the workers whom she was trying

MARY MACARTHUR.

to organize, nobody was much the worse for that. She went through the two quiet, rather sleepy rooms which the League occupied in Gray's Inn Road like a tornado. She discovered that it had been for years running on a deficit. This would not do ; she set out to make it pay its way, and by the end of her first year was able to present to her annual meeting a balance-sheet in which the balance was on the right side.

That was something, if it was not very much. But she was determined to put the League " on the map," and to get on with the job which it had been formed to do. Here her energy, her natural gifts for publicity, and her ability as a speaker helped her a great deal. She was not going to sit down and wait for men's Trade Unions and middle-class sympathizers who had money to join the League ; she was going out to compel them to do so. In two years she raised the League's membership by over twenty per cent. to 70,000.

She was not, however, spending her whole time in an office or going round asking for subscriptions. The League's job was not simply to get more money, but to use the money which it got in helping working women to help themselves. Accordingly, much of her energy went on field work outside the office, speaking to groups at factory and street corner meetings, as John Turner had once spoken to her, listening to workers' grievances and complaints, and seeing what could be done to redress them, leading deputations to managers of factories, and when the women struck, guiding and helping the strikers. Of course she was not alone in this work ; she had lieutenants who helped her, and she had an immense gift for inspiring working girls and women throughout the country with desire to help the cause that she had made her own. " I find," she said almost in surprise, " that girls get absolutely crazy about the idea of being missionaries of Trade Unionism." Crazy they may have become, but it was Mary's own tremendous enthusiasm and personal magnetism that made them so, and no one who ever worked under her will ever forget it. She was temperamental to a very high degree ; she retained, almost to the end of her life, some of the qualities of " the wild girl of the class " which she had had in her youth. She could weep, and storm, and bully ; but when all was over she had a gift for making people slave for her and her cause which few have ever possessed.

The Women's Trade Union League was growing in numbers, membership, and importance. But before very long Mary saw that by itself it was not strong enough to achieve the ends at which she and its founders were aiming. The real reason for this lay in the poverty of the women whom it was trying to organize. Apart from the Lancashire cotton trade, the average wage of all working women was somewhere between seven and eight shillings a week, and it was simply impossible for women, out of that wage, to contribute enough to keep an organization going in all the many separate trades in which they worked. Among laundry workers or tailoresses, for example, a small Union might be formed out of keen workers who would give a penny or twopence a week (twopence a week was one-fortieth of their whole income, equal to £25 out of £1,000 a year) ; but the sum thus accumulated would be very small indeed, and if there was any strike, it would not suffice to keep the strikers alive for more than a week or two.

Part of this difficulty Mary Macarthur met by the foundation, in 1906, of the National Federation of Women Workers, in which all women workers could be enrolled in whatever trade they were working. This meant that instead of a dozen or so tiny societies there was one larger society to which all the women contributed, and which, therefore, had four or five times the amount of funds available for an emergency. But even so, the combined membership was so small that it could make very little difference. The basic fact was that the majority of women workers were being paid wages so low that they could not afford to do anything to help themselves, and that the few employers who were willing to pay more were hindered by the competition of the " sweaters." * What was needed was for the Government to come to the rescue, to fix, by legislation, minimum

* " Sweating," in the industrial sense, means paying wages insufficient to provide the worker who receives them with the minimum standard of life.

wages less than which nobody would be allowed to pay their workers. But would the Government do it ?

There was a chance. The long period of Conservative domination of British politics was coming to an end, and the Liberals, who were about to win so sweeping a victory in December 1905, were pledged to do something to improve the conditions of the poorer classes. But if anything was to be done public opinion must be roused, and people with normally kind hearts must be made to see that it was a scandal that those who served them should have to live in such dire poverty.

Mary Macarthur had not been a part-time journalist for nothing. At the end of 1905 she went to see Mr. A. G. Gardiner, then editor of the *Daily News*, a paper noted for its willingness to support good causes. She argued with him, and she wept at him. Which was the most potent appeal we do not know, but the upshot was that Mr. Gardiner agreed to put the whole weight of the *Daily News* behind an exhibition of " Sweated Industries " to be held in London in 1906.

This exhibition continued throughout the summer, and judging from the numbers who attended it, the effect was enormous. Comfortably-off people had had literally no idea of the price which others paid for their comforts ; and when they saw the facts, the conditions under which the makers of artificial flowers, shirts, sacks, furs, tennis rackets, boxes, and many other commodities worked, spoke with them about it, and observed with their own eyes the amount of bread, meat, and potatoes which their wages would buy in a week, they were flabbergasted.

The worst, though by no means the only case of sweating, was among " outworkers," *i.e.* workers who took to their own homes materials supplied by the employer and made them up, often working (since there were no regulations for them) far into the night to earn a few pence by making a garment to be sold for many shillings. Superior West End houses were some of the worst offenders in this respect, and were proved to be paying 6d. and 8d. to a woman for the entire making of a blouse for which their customers would be asked 25s. or 30s., and often deducting from those rates fines for work imperfectly done. Those who bought the fine clothes had their consciences stricken by reconstructions of the hovels in which they were made.

More, indeed, than their consciences might well have been stricken, as was clearly shown by an incident which occurred a year or two later when Mary Macarthur was pleading before a Select Committee of the House of Commons which had been set up as a result of the exhibition to inquire into sweating. The Committee had asked for evidence about the making of baby linen. Mary began to investigate Press advertisements of babies' outfits, and traced one of them to the slum where it was being made—by a girl who received the sum of one penny for each garment. The girl could not afford bedclothes, and at night she covered herself with the baby clothes she was making. But she was ill of diphtheria, and Mary, through handling the garments, herself caught diphtheria and spent six weeks in hospital. As she herself said afterwards, it was worth while for the women's sake ; for many who were impervious to appeals to their humanity shivered at the thought of poverty bringing disease into their homes.

The first hurdle was surmounted. Public opinion was aroused ; the Trade Union movement, long suspicious of Government action, declared itself in favour of a legal minimum wage ; the Select Committee, stunned by the evidence which Mary and her helpers brought before them, reported in favour of legislation ; and at the end of 1909 the Government passed an Act, the Trade Boards Act, under which, for four of the worst-paid trades, chainmaking, lacemaking, paper boxes, and wholesale and bespoke tailoring,* Boards representatives of employers and employed and " impartial persons " were to fix minimum rates of pay for all classes of workers.

But there was still a great deal of the fight to come. When the Boards were set up the rates of pay had to be fixed, and the workers' representatives, who not surprisingly were for the most part inexperienced and inarticulate, had to be helped to argue their case at the meetings ; and when the rates were finally fixed, an

---

* Subsequently, though not for some years, the principle was extended to cover a good many other trades, though there are still some which ought to be included and are not.

agitation had to be set on foot to see that they were paid.

The case of the chainmakers of Cradley Heath will serve as an example. At Cradley Heath, in Staffordshire, women chainmakers, doing hard, rough, and unpleasant work, were getting from 5s. to 6s. to as much as 12s. a week if they were lucky, the lowest rent of a two-roomed house being at that time 3s. a week. After a great struggle the Trade Board fixed rates which meant a doubling of wages for the lowest paid workers. But there was a period of grace before the new rates became compulsory, and during that period, by an unfortunate clause in the Act, workers were allowed to " contract out," *i.e.* to sign a paper saying that they did not wish to be paid the new rates. At once the sweating employers became busy ; they persuaded hundreds of women and girls, too ignorant to know what they were doing, to sign contracting-out papers. At the same time they put all their employees on overtime at the old rates, piling up immense quantities of cheap chains in order that, when the appointed day came, the good employers, who were willing to pay the higher wages, would find that they could not sell their chains because the market was overstocked. They would have to close down temporarily or put their workers on short time, and thus the immediate effects of the new rates would appear to be, for the workers, unemployment and complete instead of half starvation.

There was only one thing to be done. The reputable

employers, those in the Manufacturers' Association, would agree to pay the new rates if they could be protected against undercutting by the middlemen and the outsiders. And how was that to be done? Only by a refusal to work for the undercutters, and that meant calling a strike among women who had hardly anything to live on, anyway. Could it be done? And what would they live on while they were out? Mary decided to take the risk. She went down to Cradley Heath and spoke to the women. They came out, and for ten weeks they stayed on strike, supported only by such funds as she could manage to raise by public meetings and by subscriptions from sympathisers, until at last the pressure of public opinion forced the recalcitrant employers to give way. The lowest time-rate, when the battle was over, rested at twopence three-farthings per hour; and there were a few inspectors appointed by the Government to see that it was paid.

The story of Cradley Heath has been told in detail, as an illustration; but all over the country similar struggles were proceeding, that of the Nottingham lace-workers, some of whom were paid only a penny or three-farthings per hour, being particularly severe. All through the years between 1909 and 1914 Mary Macarthur and the National Federation of Women Workers were conducting a perpetual series of campaigns for the raising of wages and the improvement of conditions in all manner of trades. For the spirit of which the Cradley Heath

strike is typical spread far beyond the industries covered
by Trade Boards. The chainmakers had won their
wages not merely by legislation, but through their own
action, and what they had done others could do. In the
years just before the war, when prices were beginning to
rise, so that the workers' wages, while no less in terms of
money, would buy less food, there was a good deal of what
was called "labour unrest"—*i.e.* strikes and demands for
better conditions—and the women, who before had been
afraid, after Cradley Heath plucked up their courage to
put in their claims.

The National Federation of Women Workers, which,
small though its actual membership was, had established
its claim—because it knew its business and its own mind
and was trusted by thousands of women who could not
afford to join it—was ready with advice and help and
leadership for any group which wanted it ; and part of
the success it had was due to the fact that Mary Macarthur
and its other leaders never forgot, when organizing a
dispute, to make their appeal to the workers and to public
opinion simultaneously. They wanted the women to
stand on their own feet and to help themselves, to get
the self-confidence and the sense of comradeship and
mutual assistance which only being organized together
for a cause can give ; but they also wanted to get sympathy from the public at large, and the material help
without which the women would not have been able to
continue. Fortunately, in one sense, the wages paid

were still so extraordinarily low that, once the facts had been published, practical sympathy was almost certain to arrive.

For instance, in August 1911, a month of great heat and of much unrest, a series of strikes for improved wages took place in the crowded and slum-filled borough of Bermondsey. The strikes started in food-producing trades, confectionery works, jam and biscuit factories, pickle factories, etc. (which must have been intolerably stifling in the heat), but rapidly spread to other trades, until thousands of women were out on the streets, with no Unions, no strike pay, and no savings. Mary Macarthur called to the scene of action to organize fifteen to twenty thousand workers and to conduct at least twenty separate strikes, wrote an appeal to the Press. " Many thousands of women," she said, " are on strike, many more are locked out, the pawnshops are closed and outdoor relief refused.

" As wages for many women in the jam, pickle, glue, and tin-box trades range from 7s. to 9s. weekly when at work, there is no margin for a crisis of this kind.

" The plight of the children is pitiable. We want at least a thousand loaves of bread at the Labour Institute, Fort Road, Bermondsey, if possible by noon on Monday. Who will send them ? "

They came—loaves, herrings, condensed milk, and money to buy more. For three weeks the Labour Institute at Fort Road presented the appearance of a beleaguered city, with women and girls, many of them with babies in their arms, standing in queues from six o'clock in the morning until nearly midnight in order to get supplies or to help to organize. At the end, wage advances had been won in eighteen out of the twenty-one disputes, and thousands of women workers had joined the Federation. It may perhaps be noted, as evidence both of the hard work that was put in during those three weeks, and of the poverty of the Federation's clients, that after the strikes were over the Labour Institute had to be officially cleared of vermin.

The story of Bermondsey was repeated in many other districts, among the Somerset collarmakers, the Bridport networkers, the Kidderminster carpet-girls, and a host of others. At the same time the introduction in 1911 of the Bill which made health insurance compulsory upon all workers had immensely increased the work falling on the National Federation—first, in discussing and arguing about the clauses of the Bill before it became an Act; secondly, in combating an attempt to leave domestic servants outside it; and thirdly, in setting up a special society within the Federation to administer it when it was passed. All this, added to her other work, and to the cares of a home, made Mary Macarthur's life more and more of a scramble.

For Mary was now a married woman, and to chronicle that we must look a little way back. She had known Will. Anderson a comparatively long time. He was a member of her own Union, the Shop Assistants. Son of a blacksmith in Banff, he had started life as a boy in a chemist's shop, and had very early in life become a Socialist and joined the Scottish Independent Labour Party, where Mary came in contact with him almost at the beginning of her career. His mind was made up almost at once ; he first asked her to marry him in 1903, when she refused, believing that for her work must come first, and that marriage would be only a distraction. Anderson, however, was not discouraged. He knew how to wait, and wait he did, until in the autumn of 1911, moved a little, it may be, by the deaths, at a very short interval, of two of her closest friends and comrades, Margaret Middleton and Margaret Macdonald,* she consented to marry him. They were married in the November, and it may be said at once that the step, though delayed, was one which she never regretted. Anderson, with his wider knowledge, deeper reading, and steadier, though less brilliant personality, provided the ballast and anchorage which her nature needed, and more and more, through the ensuing years, she was found to be relying upon his patience and judgment to carry her through her recurrent crises. Together, if disaster had not intervened, they might have combined into a formidable force against reaction.

To say that Mary Macarthur was happy in her

* Wives of J. S. Middleton, now secretary of the Labour Party, and of Ramsay Macdonald, once its chairman.

marriage, however, is not to say she was happy in her housekeeping. An excellent cook and manager herself, she had the very minimum of gift, either for conforming to method in her home life or for choosing reliable helpers. Again and again she was reduced to despairing telephone calls to her friends to come and help her out of chaos ; and matters were not assisted by the fact that she seemed incapable of distinguishing between her home and her office, so that no one could tell in which half of the house in Mecklenburgh Square, which from 1912 sheltered them both, either Mary or any property or documents of hers that were particularly wanted would be likely to be found. Added to which, she was working herself, during those early years, at a pitch which even her splendid health and vigour could not endure ; and it is not surprising that in April 1913 her son was born dead and she herself broke down. For some time she was almost incapable of public work ; and though she recovered, the recovery was slow and was barely completed by the time that the European War broke out.

Few in this generation can realize the shock with which the war came to the social workers of 1914. Nowadays we are all discussing wars and rumours of wars ; we are used to social reforms being postponed on the pleas that " national security " and the need for greater armaments make it impossible to afford them ; and if war comes, we cannot say that nobody has warned us. But in 1914 no one was anticipating war ; the world was patently growing richer as invention was proceeding, and pioneers like Mary Macarthur, looking back on the successes of the past few years, expected that things would continue to improve, that public opinion would continue to support better wages and better social organization, until poverty was a thing of the past. Instead came the war, and for a while the pioneers were stunned by the shock, until they roused themselves to deal with the problems which war brought in its train.

These were two, the first immediate but passing, and the second lasting for the duration. The immediate result of the outbreak of the war was widespread distress. Trade and business were dislocated ; workers were dismissed or put on part-time, and there was great unemployment, especially among women. Within a month of the declaration of war there were 190,000 women out of work. This emergency was met by relief measures, notably Queen Mary's Work for Women Fund, with the administration of which Mary Macarthur was closely concerned ; and as the war went on and more and more men were enrolled in the forces, the problem of unemployment disappeared and was replaced by one of a quite opposite character—the problem of women on war work.

If the men were to fight, and to fight in ever-increasing numbers, somebody had got to do the work which they had done before, to keep the country going, to provide food and clothes, both for those in the army and for those left at home. *Somebody*, moreover, had to undertake the job of making munitions, of providing guns, shells, and equipment for the millions of soldiers in the field—and these somebodies could only be women. By the beginning of 1915 it was clear that there would be an immense influx of women, first into the munitions trades, and then into all manner of jobs previously performed by men ; and the only question was : under what conditions should they be employed ?

The question was a difficult one, and four years of war did not suffice to settle it, especially as it had to be argued, for the most part, in the hysterical state of feeling which war patriotism produces. It was believed, by a great many honest and sincere persons, that to haggle about your pay and your hours of work when the existence of the country was at stake was unpatriotic and abominable ; and the very same people (such is human nature) who made speeches on public platforms saying that " the women are wonderful " were quite capable of shrieking with rage, in their private capacity, when the same women's leaders suggested that, if they were as wonderful as that, they were worthy of receiving, as war prices rose and rose, a minimum of sixpence an hour, decent working conditions in the factories, and a working day short enough to leave them with some vitality when it was over. It does not sound much to ask, but it was a long time before those in authority realized that these demands were sensible as well as just.

For, in spite of all that the Trade Boards and the N.F.W.W. had done, over large tracts of industry the old bad tradition of starvation wages for women prevailed, and the great rush into industry of women and girls who had never worked for wages before and who did not know what organization meant made it easy enough to pay them the lowest possible rates. There were plenty of engineering and other firms who were glad enough to " release their male workers for the colours," and, at the price of a little extra money spent on supervision, to replace them by women earning from one-half downwards of the men's former rates, thus combining patriotism with profit in the most pleasing way.

It was through this " dilution," as the substitution of women for men, particularly in engineering, was called, that Mary Macarthur and the National Federation of Women Workers were enabled to stem the rot. For the skilled men who joined the army and who, through many years of apprenticeship and organization, had succeeded in achieving a standard rate of pay for their own jobs, were not unnaturally apprehensive at seeing their places taken by women at very much lower pay. What was to happen when the war was over, or when they individually were discharged from the army? Would the employers be so contented with their new cheap labour that they would decide to keep on employing it ? And if so, where would the men be, and how would they live ? Not even the longest war can last for ever, and those who were fortunate enough to survive would have to make a livelihood when they came home.

The skilled men were alarmed ; their Unions were alarmed on their behalf, and were prepared to resist dilution unless satisfactory terms could be arranged. With them Mary Macarthur, speaking for the National Federation of Women Workers, was in full accord. It was, as has already been said, fortunate for her that she entered the Labour Movement through a Trade Union which had never suffered from sex antagonism ; and all her work had tended to foster in her the conviction that there was no real difference of interests between men and women in industry, that where there appeared to be it was because the system, by underpaying the women, had turned them into competitors of the men. She never made the mistake which some ardent suffragists made, who were so delighted that women should show that they could do " men's work " that they never considered either at what price they were doing it or what effect it would have on society. Thus she succeeded, not without considerable argument at times—for men as well as women can be short-sighted—in joining forces with the men's Trade Unions, notably the Amalgamated Society of Engineers. The understood, if not always expressed, basis of co-operation was that the women would promise to give up their jobs when the men came home, that the men would support the women's claim to a living wage in the meantime, and that both sides would press for decent conditions and for reasonable hours of work.

On the whole, the partnership was successful, though it involved endless struggles of a kind which it would be tedious to describe, but which recall vividly the struggles over the Trade Boards, both to get minimum rates established and to force recalcitrant firms to pay them. On one occasion at least, in Glasgow, it was necessary to threaten strike action before the rates prescribed by the Government itself could be secured. And it must be remembered that all this agitation and bargaining had to take place in the hectic atmosphere of war-time, when anybody who seemed for a moment to be holding up the supply of munitions was always likely to be mobbed by an unthinking crowd, or attacked as a traitor in the Press.

Looking back upon it afterwards, there were few who would not admit that the campaign for better wages and conditions was right. Even during the war itself, a responsible Government Committee came to the conclusion that to underfeed munition workers, to make them work a twelve-hour day in insanitary factories with no proper provision for meals or for washing, did not pay even in the short run, however patriotic it might be thought. As Edith Cavell said (though she was probably not thinking of munition workers), " Patriotism is not enough," *i.e.* during a protracted struggle it will pay better to be reasonable, and to think things out, rather than to trust to the unchecked dictates of emotion.

But at the time it needed a cool head and a con-viction of the essential rightness of one's line of approach to enable one to stick to it. Both of these Mary Macarthur possessed. Though her manner was often emotional and her language intemperate, she had plenty of judgment, and she could hold fast to the point she intended to win ; and she could use her power of emotional appeal to very good purpose in winning it. (Part of the antagonism which she always felt towards Mr. Lloyd George was no doubt due to the fact that they possessed much the same qualities. They were rival spellbinders ; but he, as Minister of Munitions, was inevitably on many occasions her antagonist. And Mary did not like him at all.)

She did not achieve the full aim which she had set herself—equal pay for men and women on munition work. The rush of patriotic women to the factories, combined with the tradition which to this day, except in a very few occupations like medicine, ordains that, whatever the merit of a woman's work, she shall be paid less than a man, was too strong for her. But she did secure that minimum standards were laid down, and that special tribunals (which did a great deal of valuable work) were set up to look after their enforcement. Her war-time experiences, also, made her into a considerable public figure, since she and Miss Gertrude Tuckwell (for many years the ardent Honorary Secretary of the Women's Trade Union League) had by dint of steady service and persistent agitation, made themselves recognized as the representatives of the working women of Great Britain. In this capacity, and perhaps not un-helped by the fact that she had become acquainted with Queen Mary in the early days of the war, Mary Macarthur was received and encouraged in what is commonly called " Society." Here, however, her Highland blood stood her in good stead, for there is no snobbery among the Highlanders. She was amused and interested ; she was a " good mixer," and she liked parties and gatherings, and to be able to impress them when she made a speech. But her head was never turned to any degree ; she knew where her heart was and where her comrades were. All that was happening was that she was getting experience to enable her to function on a wider stage—if she had lived to do it.

The war drew to its close. Every one was hopeful at the time of the Armistice ; every one was remembering Mr. Lloyd George's speeches about a new world and homes for heroes, and President Wilson's stipulations about a League of Nations and the humanizing of inter-national relations. The Labour movement, including Mary Macarthur and her friends, prepared for the imminent general election with high hopes. It was of peculiar interest to them, because an Act of Parliament, passed a few months previously, had given to women, for the first time, the right to vote and to stand as candi-dates. The Labour Party, now become a nation-wide organizat:on, put forward women candidates, and Mary

Macarthur was the first (actually the first woman candidate in the whole of England) to be adopted. The constituency which selected her was Stourbridge in Worcestershire, where the voters included a number of the chainmakers and hollow-ware makers for whom she had fought in the early days of the Trade Boards. Will. Anderson was defending his own seat—supposed at the time to be perfectly safe—at Attercliffe in Sheffield.

Almost at once an unexpected hindrance appeared. When Mary married, though according to English law her name changed, she had in practice not altered it. The women whom she had served knew her as Mary Macarthur, and she was not going to confuse their allegiance by turning up under a different name. But when she came to stand for Parliament, she found that the law, in the person of the Returning Officer, was adamant. She was not Mary Macarthur, but Mary Reid Anderson, and thus her name must be printed on the ballot paper. Though, of course, all that was possible was done to explain the change of name to the electors, there is no doubt that many votes were lost because illiterate women, who had never voted before, did not realize that the unfamiliar name signified that Mary Macarthur who had been their leader and inspirer nearly ten years before.

This, however, was a minor difficulty. Quite early on it became apparent that the mood of the Armistice had passed, and had been succeeded by what we may now call the mood of Versailles. It is not very profitable to try and apportion the blame for this ; most people are now agreed that the 1918 election, which was fought on the twin slogans of " Hang the Kaiser " and " Make Germany Pay," and which resulted in the return of a Parliament pledged to exact the last possible penalty from their late enemies, was a disaster of which we are only beginning to reap the consequences. Whosesoever the fault, the fact was that every candidate who did not receive the Lloyd George coupon, or who had ever favoured the termination of the war by negotiation, was branded as a pacifist, a traitor, and a coward, and had cast against him or her all the unthinking vote which takes its instructions from the cheap Press.

Mary Macarthur went down with the rest (including the majority of the subsequent leaders of British Labour), though, considering all the circumstances, she did not do at all badly. A much heavier blow to her than her own reverse was the totally unexpected defeat of Will. Anderson at Attercliffe, which constituency had been regarded as so safe that she had not troubled to give him any assistance. But a worse blow was to come.

The result of the election was declared on 28th December, ensuring an unhappy New Year for a great many people. She and her husband, however, rallied their courage, and began to prepare new plans for dealing with the confusion which was bound to arise when the soldiers were discharged from the army and the munitions works were closed down. But in January and

February the appalling influenza epidemic broke over Europe. It was no less lethal than the plagues of which we read in history. Whole families were stricken, and the medical and nursing services gave way under the strain. On 16th February Will Anderson came home chilled after a meeting at Bradford ; the illness rapidly developed, and for some days no nurse could be obtained. On the 25th he died.

With his death the mainspring went out of Mary's life. In seven years she had grown to trust him and to depend upon him in a way of which the girl who had refused to marry him " because her work came first " could scarcely have dreamed. It is true that she rallied after the first shock ; but the short remainder of her life reads like an epilogue.

Later in the year she paid a visit to America, where she spoke passionately in favour of a real peace and against the Versailles Treaty, whose shocking terms were just beginning to filter through to the public. Shortly after her return she was asked to be a delegate to the first (Washington) Conference of the International Labour Organization, at which a number of international agreements for the protection of the workers were drawn up, some of which—though by no means all—are in operation to-day. Her chief interest, while she was there, was in a Convention for the payment of allowances to working women before and after the birth of children, so that they could rest without fear of starvation. (This is one of the Conventions which is not yet in operation in this country.) While she was actually in America she seemed to be in possession of her old vigour, to such an extent even that the head of the British delegation was forced to discipline her, and to point out that she was not appearing as an individual, but as a member of a group, and must not attempt to play a lone hand. But she was ill on the way home, possibly owing to a lift accident which befell her in New York, and shortly after she returned it became clear that an operation would be necessary. The operation was only successful for a time; in the autumn of 1920 it became clear that another would have to be performed.

In the meantime she had put through a piece of reorganization which, not very epoch-making in itself, is yet so much in accordance with her whole policy that it is peculiarly fitting as her last public act. She had always believed in the common interests of men and women workers, and in the summer of 1920, in connection with the reorganization of the Trades Union Congress, she carried through the incorporation of the body which she had founded, the National Federation of Women Workers, as a section of the National Union of General Workers, which catered for both men and women. At the same time she secured that women should have representation on the new governing body of the Trade Union movement.

The Trades Union Congress of September 1920 was

her last public appearance of any importance. In October she underwent a second operation, and died on New Year's Day 1921 little past her fortieth birthday.

"I cannot think," she wrote to the N.F.W.W. only a little while before her death, "of a greater happiness to wish my own child * than that she should, like me, be enabled to spend herself fully and freely in the cause of an ideal in which she believes."

* Her daughter Nancy Anderson.

ELIZABETH GARRETT ANDERSON

V

ELIZABETH GARRETT ANDERSON

ELIZABETH GARRETT ANDERSON, who died in 1917, is generally counted the first English woman doctor ; for Dr. Elizabeth Blackwell, who was actually the first woman to succeed in obtaining an English medical degree, lived and practised mainly in the United States. The hard work which had to be done in partly opening the medical profession to women —only partly, for even now a number of medical schools refuse to admit women as their pupils—was done by Elizabeth Garrett Anderson and her younger contemporary Sophia Jex-Blake.

Elizabeth was born in 1836. She was the second daughter of Newsom Garrett, merchant, who owned a small fleet of trading vessels which plied between Aldeburgh in Suffolk, where Mr. Garrett and his family lived, and London, and also made voyages to Newcastle and the north. In those days Aldeburgh was primarily a fishing and seafaring town, and hardly to any extent a pleasure resort. It was not easy of access ; even after

Elizabeth was twenty the nearest railway station was at Ipswich, twenty-eight miles away, so that a journey to London, to see the Great Exhibition of 1851, for example, for which the Crystal Palace was built in Hyde Park, was very much of an event. Yet Aldeburgh was an old town of distinction ; it had two bailiffs and an ancient corporation, and silver maces which had been kept in the Moot Hall since the time of Queen Elizabeth ; it held in considerable reverence its own distinguished poet George Crabbe—his house has since been pulled down— and it had a number of families of some consequence living in the neighbourhood. It paid less attention to its poorer citizens ; though the labouring men of Aldeburgh and the neighbourhood provided the power which manned the ships and caught the fish, even a man who respected and got on with them as well as Mr. Garrett did not think it necessary, for example, to see that they had any education. Even in the sixties Aldeburgh, like many other places of its size up and down the country, made absolutely no provision for the education of those who could not afford expensive school fees.

Newsom Garrett did not come of the landed aristocracy, but of that yeoman stock which was for generations so strong in rich agricultural countries like Suffolk, and still persists enough to make the people of East Anglia less mixed in their origins than those of the Midlands or southern England. His ancestors on both sides had for years played their part as small landowners, master craftsmen, or even skilled artisans. His father had a small machinery works at Leiston, in the early days of the Industrial Revolution ; one of his brothers took it on, and it is still there, somewhat enlarged since those early days and now making tractors and steam rollers. Some of Newsom Garrett's relations might have thought it not inappropriate that he should be remotely connected with a steam roller.

For he was a man of a type which seems to have been fairly common in early Victorian England—a man of enormous energy and inventiveness, always tearing about the country and taking up new pastimes and occupations. He was prominent, for instance, in the saving of life at sea, for which there was ample opportunity on the treacherous Suffolk coast, whose shoals and sandbanks and easterly gales are quite as dangerous to shipping, though they make a less spectacular show, than the fierce rocks and roaring breakers of the west. His children were immensely proud of a vellum certificate— still in existence—which records :

" That the special thanks of the Royal National Lifeboat Association be presented to Newsom Garrett, Esq., in testimony of his highly meritorious conduct in assisting to rescue through the surf nine out of the eleven of the crew of the Swedish brig *Vesta*, which in a gale of wind was wrecked near Orford Low Lighthouse on the 2nd November 1855."

135

On land he was possibly less happy. He was extremely fond of driving and somewhat prone to make straight for his destination, ignoring such minor obstacles as the absence of a road. He was, therefore, frequently upset, though never seriously hurt ; and his family became used to seeing his horse arrive home without him, and did not leap to the conclusion that he had broken his neck. Even in old age, when he could not get about well and was reduced to a bath-chair drawn by an elderly pony, even this he managed to upset, and was found, as his daughter Mrs. Fawcett related, " laughing to himself, the pony standing perfectly quiet, my father still encased in his wrappings, chair and all, like a hermit crab in its shell."

As regards the innovating side of his character, as soon as Turkish baths were invented he built himself one at Alde House. A groom, watching its construction, was heard to grumble, " Master is buildin' himself a sweatin' house : if he'd rub the horses down he wouldn't need no sweatin' house "—and, though long a Conservative in politics, he welcomed any innovation in economic life, even the coming of the railway which destroyed much of the carrying trade of his ships.

As one would expect, both from these characteristics and from the time at which he lived, he was a vigorous controversialist who was far from living at peace with his neighbours. Both his daughter Elizabeth and her younger sister Millicent (who afterwards became Mrs. Fawcett)

DR. ELIZABETH GARRETT ANDERSON,
after the portrait by John Sargent.

shared with him the trait of believing that they were entirely right and everybody who disagreed with them in the wrong, and of saying so in somewhat unmeasured language. His wife, who managed him perhaps more than he was aware, often had her work cut out to sympathize with his disputes without being involved in them. Nevertheless, he was not in any sense the domestic tyrant that many men like him became ; he had a power of respecting other people even when he differed from them violently, and he was always helpful and generous in aiding young men towards a career. We shall see later how invaluable was the support which he gave to his daughter Elizabeth, against her mother's wishes, in a struggle which was bound to involve her in tremendous unpopularity.

In Alde House at Aldeburgh, then a high, rambling, creeper-covered building, Elizabeth and her nine brothers and sisters—it was a real Victorian family—were brought up, the close contact with the sea, and farming, and their father's ships partly making up for deficiencies in their early education, for in common with other Victorian young ladies they had at first only a governess, a Miss Edgeworth, who taught them as well as she could, but knew in fact very little more than they did, and was quite incompetent to teach it. However, Newsom Garrett had more generous ideas about the education of women than many Victorian parents, and his daughters were soon sent to a school at Blackheath kept by a Miss

Louisa Browning, aunt of Robert Browning the poet, where Elizabeth stayed until she was fifteen, which was generally thought to be quite long enough for a girl to go on being educated. Then she was sent on a foreign tour to be what was called " finished."

Miss Louisa Browning's school might not nowadays win the approval of every educationist, because she had views and opinions of her own as to what ought to be taught to girls and how—she violently objected, among other idiosyncracies, to any one bringing needlework into her school, believing that it ought to be done at home. And, as she was not hampered by having to " prepare for examinations," she could, in fact, do what she liked. But she was a born teacher, as well as a strong if eccentric personality ; and Elizabeth and her sisters retained all their lives a vivid impression of this massive lady, her large person clothed in scarlet, purple, yellow, and green at once—for she had an affection for bright colours—ruling her pupils with a rod of iron. (She stated, after the death of Elizabeth Barrett Browning, that she had a black dress upstairs, " in case Robert should happen to call," but it seems he never did ; at least, no one ever saw the black dress.)

More important, in its results upon Elizabeth's future life, than anything she learned with Miss Browning was the friendship she and her elder sister made there with two girls called Crowe, who lived in the north of England. Their friendship was kept up after she had left school and became a " young lady," and in 1854, while on a visit to the Crowes, she met another young lady, six years older than herself and daughter of a clergyman, whose name was Emily Davies. A friendship began which progressed rapidly, as Elizabeth Garrett found that with Emily Davies she could hold a great many discussions on the sort of political and social questions with which her developing mind was beginning to busy itself ; and the result, though not until a few years had passed, was that Elizabeth Garrett announced to her surprised and alarmed family her intention of becoming a doctor.

Well might they be both alarmed and surprised. For not only was the process of becoming a doctor, at that time, likely to be very long, disheartening, and thoroughly unpleasant, even if she did finally succeed, as seemed very doubtful : they were also entitled to remark that they had never been given any hint that such an idea was in the offing, and that Elizabeth had not during all her previous life—she was twenty-one when the idea was finally formulated—shown any particular sign of possessing a vocation for medicine. This on the whole was true. Elizabeth had not noticeably displayed any of the qualities which are supposed to indicate a medical bent ; she was not particularly interested in science, or in the art of healing, or in sick persons. She was not like Florence Nightingale, whose passion for nursing ought to have been obvious to any but the most bat-eyed relatives from her earliest childhood ; indeed, Mrs. Naomi

Mitchison, who wrote a very interesting sketch of Elizabeth Garrett in a book called *Revaluations*, suggests that she was not a born doctor, nor, in fact, an especially good doctor. Whether or not she became a good doctor—and, in fact, she was a successful one—there is at any rate sufficient doubt about her vocation to make one inquire why she should have hit on that particular career. The answer is in two words—Emily Davies. Emily Davies decided that her friend should become a doctor, and a doctor she in due course became.

To understand why Emily Davies set her on that path one must understand something about the position of Englishwomen of the middle class in the early and mid-nineteenth century. The nineteenth century, *i.e.* the period following the beginning of what we have learned to call the industrial revolution, was, if we consider it for the moment simply from the standpoint of women, a very peculiar time. On the one hand, the introduction of machinery into manufacture, particularly textile manufacture, had, by putting mechanical power in the place of human muscles, made it possible for women, and even for girls and children, to do a great deal of factory work which had hitherto been only possible for men. As women and girls received much lower rates of wages than men, it paid the factory owners to employ them, and the result, therefore, of the industrial revolution on poor women and poor girls was to make many of them work much harder, under abominable conditions, for miserably low wages. What this meant in practice you can see from the chapter on Mary Macarthur in this book.

The result for the middle or respectable classes—the classes which would under no circumstances have gone in for factory work—was rather different. In fact, so far from the industrial revolution making the middle-class woman work harder, it tended rather to keep her in complete idleness. For this reason.

Before machinery and machine products came into general use, the women of the middle-class household were no less busy—though they did not earn money—than the men. So many things which nowadays can be bought at a shop (sometimes in a tin) had to be made in the home, and so many services which we now pay outside firms to perform for us were of necessity organized there (as on many farms they were until much later) that there was no scarcity of jobs. Comparatively few households nowadays make all their own jams, pickles, and preserved fruits, bake their own bread, buns, and biscuits, do their own laundry, and make all their own clothes, sheets, and household goods ; it is so much cheaper and easier to pay some one else for all these things. But at the beginning of the nineteenth century they did, and it was the woman who was responsible for getting them all done ; and as they were thus occupied, the women, as a whole, had little time or inclination, unless something went wrong, to take notice of the fact that they were, in the eyes of the law, in a position definitely inferior to that of the men, that they had no voice or vote in the way in which that law was made or administered, and that, once married, they had practically no right at all against their husbands. It was only exceptionally intelligent women, with a strong sense of abstract justice, like Mary Wollstonecraft, or women who had been very badly treated by their husbands, like Caroline Norton, who protested ; and nobody took any particular notice of their protests. They were regarded as insane, or immoral, or, at best, very unfortunate persons for whom allowances had to be made.

As the industrial revolution proceeded, however, more and more of women's work in the home was taken over by shops and factories, and the women of the comfortable classes came to have less and less to do. And as the more money the man made, the more he could afford to buy of the shop and factory products, it came to be a sign of wealth and respectability to be able to keep your wife and daughters in complete idleness, buying them clothes and jewels, etc., which they could wear in order to advertise to all comers that you were very well-off indeed. In former days men showed off their wealth on their own persons by dressing in fine clothes and expensive materials. Early Victorian men could not dress up themselves, but they could buy thousand-pound necklaces and hang them on their wives' necks, making the wives a kind of shop-window in which they could display their own wealth. And they could keep their wives' hands white and their persons delicate by forbidding them to do any work which somebody else could be paid to do for them.

There are, of course, a number of people in any stage of civilization—they include men as well as women—who like to be of no use whatever, who enjoy being kept in complete idleness and spending their days in dressing and undressing, going out to tea, eating sweets and reading bad novels and goodness knows what. But the human race is not entirely composed of nit-wits, and during the nineteenth century there were a good many middle-class women who found such a prospect intolerably tedious. If there was no real and interesting work for them to do in the home they wanted to find some work outside. Some, like Florence Nightingale, whose diaries show most clearly how miserably and intolerably *boring* was the life of a society young lady who did not enjoy society, knew exactly what they wanted to do, if only they were allowed ; others were not quite so certain, but were certain that they wanted to have a job of some sort, and to feel that they were doing something that was worth while.

At once they found enormous difficulties in the way. For one thing, they did not know how to do other jobs ; they were untrained and uneducated, and nobody would train or educate them. There were no women's colleges, or good girls' schools, and the examinations which would admit to professions were for the most part only open to men. Then the men in general were opposed to their aspirations. Not only did many of them, as I have said, like the idea of being rich enough to keep their women in idleness ; there was also a good deal of unthinking contempt and sheer jealousy shown. It would have been difficult enough, in the days when middle-class women were supposed to be so frail and timid that they could hardly be seen in the streets by themselves, and certainly not in a public vehicle, for them to obtain training and employment ; it was doubly hard when men, backed up by those women who were not bored by idleness and did not want work, solidly and actively tried to prevent them.

Women, of course, who did not possess independent incomes were entirely in the power of their fathers or brothers or whatever man had the privilege of keeping them ; and when they were married, until after the passing of the Married Women's Property Act, they could have no money or property of their own unless it was specifically settled on them by law, *i.e.* if they earned or were given anything, it became the property not of themselves but of their husbands ; which meant, as divorce was almost impossible, that they could never have the use of it at all except with their husbands' consent. Mrs. Fawcett, in her autobiography, tells the story of a meeting of countrymen whom she addressed when she was trying to collect support for the Married Women's Property Bill, which afterwards became law— and finding very little. " Am I to understand you, ma'am," said one old farmer, " that if this Bill becomes law and my wife had a matter of a hundred pounds left her, I should have to *arst* her for it ? " Such was a common male attitude ; even Mrs. Fawcett herself, who had no personal complaint against her own husband, felt outraged when, on appearing in court at the trial of a man who had picked her pocket, she discovered that he was charged with " stealing from the body of Millicent Garrett Fawcett a purse, the property of Henry Fawcett " !

Finally, of course, there was the fact that whatever the feelings of women about the state of the law in these and in other matters, they could do nothing directly to alter it. The legal position of women has changed so much since 1850, and women have had the vote for so long without the skies falling, that we are apt sometimes to wonder what the suffragettes, whose exploits filled the newspapers just before the war, were making all that fuss about. Votes do not interest people so much nowadays. The answer is that Votes for Women was only a small part of the Women's Movement, which was made up of a passionate protest against *all* the disabilities and injustices which I have mentioned above, although there was something so naïvely insulting in the refusal to any woman of the voting right which nearly all men, after 1885, had as a matter of course that it aroused particular resentment, especially as this deprivation was so often presented as being in the women's own best interests. The great Mr. Gladstone, in a letter written in the eighties, announced that in his opinion to allow women to vote " would trespass upon their delicacy, their purity, their refinement, the elevation of their whole nature." As only a few years before the same statesman had been asking women to canvass for him in his Midlothian campaign without feeling that that would trespass upon their delicacy, it is hardly surprising if the women to whom the second letter referred found it peculiarly exasperating. Long before that time, however, certain of the women who felt their position most strongly had leagued themselves together to redress it, not unhelped by some of the more honest and courageous of the men, such as John Stuart Mill, who quite early put his great prestige as a Radical thinker at the service of the Women's Movement. Among the leaders of this movement was Emily Davies.

Emily Davies, who later became the first Mistress of Girton College, Cambridge, and died in 1921 at the age of ninety-one, was in many ways very unlike her predecessors in the work of feminine agitation. She was not in the least wild or alarming ; she had no awkward personal grievances or extraordinary views on morals ; she did not want a divorce, or possess a husband who drank or beat her ; and she was not " brilliant "—a very dangerous thing to be when you are arguing with men. Sophia Jex-Blake, who had remarkable brains and a tongue which she would not or could not control, hampered herself a great deal in her struggle to get the

Scottish Medical Schools to admit her because she could not refrain from scoring off her male opponents.

Emily Davies was a rector's daughter of impeccable views and modest manners. She was very small, which was in itself an asset, because it aroused men's chivalrous instincts until they discovered that besides being very small she was also very persistent. Persistence and determination, indeed, were her main qualifications. She had no intention of being beaten, and she had also some of the qualities of generalship ; at least, she could see what people were capable of being useful to her campaign, and what they could do for it. Very soon, she had marked down Elizabeth Garrett as being a highly suitable recruit, and as she was older, better informed, and very well able to marshal her arguments, she quite soon gained a considerable influence over the younger girl. Their friendship, once made, lasted until Elizabeth's death ; but all the time, it would appear from their correspondence, Emily saw herself rather in the position of guide and instructress, bound to admonish Elizabeth if she was careless or frivolous or deviated from the way of life which Emily thought suitable. A sense of humour was not Emily's strong point—perhaps she would have been less effective if it had been. Nor was she altogether popular with Emily's younger brothers and sisters. They were no fonder than most children of being lectured ; and they found in Emily Davies a young woman who took up a great deal of their big sister's time, and lectured them on political and social subjects in which they were not interested. It is possible that they disliked even more having Emily's very decided opinions thrust on them at second-hand through Elizabeth's mouth.

Anyhow, their disapproval did not affect Elizabeth seriously or interfere with Emily Davies's choice of her career. In 1859 she paid a visit to London, as she frequently did, to stay with her married elder sister. In the previous year a journal called the *Englishwoman's Journal* had been founded, largely through the efforts of another young woman, Barbara Leigh Smith, recently married to a Frenchman called Dr. Bodichon.

Barbara Leigh Smith, whose portrait now hangs in Girton College Hall, was among the most delightful characters of the early feminist movement. Her father was a remarkable man for his times, for he thought that daughters should be treated equally with sons, especially in matters of finance. He did not adopt the ordinary practice of paying their dress bills, allowing them a little pocket-money and occasionally making them a present ; he gave Barbara, from the time she came of age, an allowance of £300 a year, and exercised no control over how she spent it. She spent a good deal on painting, for she was an enthusiastic artist of ability ; but she spent it also upon the promotion of causes among women, and spent it, moreover, with a gaiety and cheerfulness which did perhaps more than the actual money to further the cause. A good many of these pioneer women strike us, on looking back, as a trifle grim and grumpy, not to say frumpy. Madame Bodichon was always light-hearted ; she dressed herself in clothes which were both comfortable and beautiful, instead of the current women's clothes which were neither ; in after years jaded Girton students, worn out with working for examinations, were sent to visit her in her country home at Robertsbridge, and almost invariably came away soothed and delighted by its free and happy atmosphere. She was one of the fortunate people who did not have to struggle painfully, as did her cousin Florence Nightingale, both with her environment and with doubts and difficulties in her own heart. Therefore she could be both convinced and carefree. " I have," wrote another cousin after a visit to her, " never come across a woman who was so much of a *citizen*."

Barbara Bodichon, then, who had made something of a name for herself by writing and publishing a little book called *Brief Summary in Plain Language of the Most Important Laws concerning Women*, had in 1858 founded the *English-woman's Journal*, from which grew a series of lectures and discussions and a little society, the Society for Women's Employment, at which classes were arranged to fit women for the occupations which they desired to take up. To one of the gatherings arranged by Madame Bodichon and her friends, in the year 1859, Dr. Elizabeth Blackwell, over from the United States, gave three lectures on medicine as a career for women.

It may seem a very small thing nowadays for women

to form a society and speak at meetings, but in those days it was not. Quite apart from the difficulties of going about alone, and so getting to the meeting at all, which I have mentioned above, there was the further difficulty of making a public appearance, standing on a platform and being stared at, especially by men. Nice women did not do these things ; nice women were brought by their husbands or brothers to meetings which were suitable for them to attend, and if they had suggestions to make, they did not get up and squeak them out in public, but whispered them in the ears of the husband or brothers, who then, if they thought fit, proclaimed them aloud. And not-so-nice women, who wanted to get a chance of occupations and careers, did not want to lessen their chances by appearing bold and immodest. (It was one of Elizabeth Garrett's advantages that, while she was not afraid of speaking, she had in youth an amiable and receptive appearance. "She looked exactly like one of the girls," Emily Davies once wrote, "whose instinct is always to do what you tell them.")

The efforts of the women were not by any means made easier, it should be noted, by the attitude of their Sovereign. Queen Victoria did not like the idea of women's emancipation ; and as the movement began to grow she liked it less and less.

"The Queen," she wrote in a letter to Theodore Martin, "the Queen is most anxious to enlist every one who can speak or write to join in checking this mad, wicked folly of ' Woman's Rights,' *with all its attendant horrors*, on which her poor feeble sex is bent, forgetting every sense of womanly feeling and propriety. . . . It is a subject which makes the Queen so *furious* that she cannot contain herself. Woman would become the most hateful, heartless, and disgusting of human beings were she allowed to unsex herself ; and where would be the protection which man was intended to give the weaker sex ? The Queen is sure that Mrs. Martin agrees with her." Mrs. Martin had better, in fact. Queen Victoria was quite frequently made " furious " by events and by persons ; and she never, as far as one can see, made any efforts to " contain herself." Apparently, however, she thought that her subjects should ; and undoubtedly her opinions, as the first lady in the land, carried a good deal of weight.

It was not until a little while later that Elizabeth, under pressure from Emily Davies, decided that she would become a doctor, and began to study Latin in order to qualify for it. Then, of course, the difficulties began.

The first was with her family, but that was not very formidable. Her mother was very much horrified and upset ; she could not bear the idea of Elizabeth's having anything to do with the physical side of medicine, especially anatomy and dissection. (That idea, the idea that women were fit to nurse all diseases, including surgical cases, but would be unsexed if they knew anything about their causes, died very hard. It is not so very long since women were denied entrance to the dissecting-rooms at Oxford.) Her father, however, when he had satisfied himself that it was not just a passing fancy, and that his Elizabeth was not likely to settle down to be a polite young lady in a drawing-room, gave way. And he did not only give way ; he proceeded to do what he could to help her to get a training.

It was not easy. Medical degrees, and the medical schools, were not open to women. In 1858 the British Medical Association, alarmed by the action of Dr. Blackwell, who had obtained her degree in America, and showed signs of practising in Great Britain, obtained an Act of Parliament which declared that no foreign qualifications would in future be recognized for British practice. It was possible that the Society of Apothecaries might grant Elizabeth a certificate, but how was she to get the training ?

Would a doctor take her as apprentice ? She approached several who seemed sympathetic, but none of them would do what she wanted—possibly they were afraid of the opinion of their fellow-practitioners. At last a Dr. William Hawes, of the Middlesex Hospital, showed himself faintly less cautious. After warning her solemnly against the horrors of her chosen career he allowed her to spend six months as a probationer-nurse at the Middlesex in order to see what she made of it.

In the autumn of 1859, therefore, being then twenty-three, she began life as a probationer. She worked in two surgical wards from eight to four every day, picking up such information and instruction as she could from doctors and nurses and students, and in the evening she studied Latin and mathematics. From the first she was keenly interested and happy in her work, and she seems to have got on and interested the teachers in herself. For she was allowed, if she gave a donation—not a fee, for that would have implied recognizing her as a student —to stay on at the hospital, getting what instruction she could ; and one of the professors offered to teach her chemistry and anatomy as a private pupil, visiting her for this purpose at her sister's house. There was some doubt whether this was really proper ; however, Emily Davies at length advised her to risk it. In 1861 she was actually admitted to lectures on chemistry and later to the dissecting-room.

But her very success militated against her. Medical students were then what, to their shame, some of them still are ; and when it became clear that Elizabeth Garrett was likely to do really well, and possibly to open the field to more women, they rose up against her. The students of the Middlesex presented a memorial, and it was decided that she must not attend any more lectures or classes there. Applications to others of the London hospitals only produced refusals, in some cases accompanied by a letter pointing out that as medical examinations were not open to women, if they admitted her to their classes they would only be providing her with the means whereby to practise illegally—which, of course, would be very scandalous of them. It was all very discouraging ; and she was not much cheered even by a letter from the Society of Apothecaries, which arrived in the summer of 1861, informing her rather grudgingly that, as far as they could see, the terms of their charter would force them to admit her to their examinations and grant her their certificate if she passed. This would give her a licence to practise—but how was she to get the necessary clinical experience ? Besides, she wanted her M.D., not a sort of poor relation of it.

The clinical work she got in the end by the somewhat unsatisfactory expedient of attending various hospitals as a nurse, struggling all the while against students and doctors who wanted to keep her out ; and by that and by hard work she succeeded in passing her examination in 1865. (It must be admitted that it was not a difficult examination.) In order to get her M.D. she tried first to pass the matriculation examination of the University of London ; and some of the girls who annually sigh their way through the papers of Matric. may feel a regret that they were not alive in 1861, when the Senate of the University, by a majority of one, rejected the application of Elizabeth Garrett to be examined for matriculation. In 1868 the Society of Apothecaries, shocked, one imagines, at the use to which their charter had been put, made a rule that they would not examine any candidate who had not come to them through the ordinary medical schools —in which women were not allowed. So that door was barred again.

Nevertheless, the opposition was nearing its end. Certificate in hand, Elizabeth Garrett opened a dispensary for women and children in the Marylebone Road, which is now the Garrett Anderson Hospital ; and she started a private practice, which grew fast, for, whatever the medical students might think, there were plenty of people who wanted to go to a woman doctor. In 1870 she got her M.D. in Paris, and in 1872 the British Medical Association elected her a member. Meanwhile the long fight of Sophia Jex-Blake for recognition from the Scottish medical schools was nearing its end ; and deciding on a change of scene, she came to London, and in 1874 founded the London School of Medicine for Women. Elizabeth Garrett joined the staff as lecturer. Even so, at first the students had to do without hospital work or the prospect of degrees, but shortly afterwards the Royal Free Hospital opened its doors to women students, and in 1876 an Act of Parliament allowed any medical school to grant degrees to women. The fight was virtually won, though some of the schools were very slow to avail themselves of the permission, and even to-day there are many restrictions on the admission of women students to hospitals.

In those days any one who was concerned in any aspect of the struggle for women's rights was bound to be a good deal in the public eye ; and as Elizabeth Garrett was also interested in many other things beside her own job, and had been brought up in a family and with friends who believed in discussing and taking an interest in political affairs, she had already become something of a public figure. She took part—naturally, as Emily Davies was her friend—in the various efforts to improve girls' education ; and she was early brought into the Women's Suffrage Movement of which her much younger sister Millicent was so long a pillar. She became a friend of John Stuart Mill's ; and when, just before the Reform Act of 1867, John Stuart Mill had promised to present the first Women's Suffrage petition to Parliament, she and Emily Davies were given the task of taking it to Westminster.

Petitions are bulky things, and the two women, having brought it in a cab to the door of the Houses of Parliament, found it so embarrassing while they waited, walking up and down while somebody went to fetch Mill, that at last they begged an old apple-woman to hide it behind her stall. When Mill at length appeared, no petition was to be seen, and " E. Garrett, choking with suppressed laughter, said, ' We've p-put it down.' " However, Mill quickly recovered it, and marched into the House brandishing it with great effect.

In 1870 the Government for the first time introduced public elementary education into England, which meant that School Boards had to be elected in all the towns to manage the schools. Elizabeth Garrett stood for the London School Board with great success. The fruits of her public work were being garnered ; the Liberals and Radicals were all in her favour, and she was loyally supported by the recently enfranchised working men for whose wives and children she had done so much both in her hospital and as private patients. When the poll was declared she stood at the top, with the largest majority of any candidate in London, having 13,000 votes more than the great Huxley. By the end of the year she was engaged to one of her staunchest supporters, M. J. G. S. Anderson, of the Skelton steamship line.

Thereafter there is not a great deal that needs to be told of Elizabeth Garrett Anderson's life. She had won through her early struggles, and had only to go on from strength to strength until, as the years went on and she felt herself growing older, she retired more and more from active work in London to the old family home in Aldeburgh, which she had inherited under her father's will, there to take up a position of lady squiress, and twice to be Mayor of Aldeburgh. All her life she retained a fresh forcefulness of manner, sometimes amounting to impatience, which reminds one more than once of the steam-roller qualities of her father. Popular as a doctor, she was not guilty of unnecessary tactfulness towards her patients. It is told that, after she had listened for a long time to the woes of a *malade imaginaire*, she rose, and after solemnly taking the flowers out of a vase which stood on the table, poured the water down her patient's neck, thereby curing that patient of any further desire to consult doctors ; and again that, having looked into the eyes of a patient with long and flattering interest, she observed with satisfaction, " Yes ! your eyebrows *are* painted." Perhaps, however, the most characteristic story is of her trying to buy a baby. To her youngest and favourite brother Sam, after several sons, there was born a girl. Only a few days after the birth, Elizabeth appeared in Sam's office and suggested that she should buy the baby for five hundred pounds down. She explained that she wanted a girl to train properly for a medical career. As she was now over fifty, she could not have another daughter of her own, and she did not want to adopt any chance child. But Sam's wife, she explained, was young, and could produce plenty more girls if they were required. She was astonished when the offer was refused ; and our later glimpses of her are of the same kind : abusing vegetarians for being faddy, telling George Meredith in his old age that he was " a very obstinate old man," and explaining to Edward VII. that he was wrong not to like her hat. She died in December 1917, having seen both her daughter and her son attain to positions of importance.

This sketch of Elizabeth Garrett Anderson has necessarily omitted a good deal. The most interesting fact, perhaps, about her life is its fullness and variety. She was not a " dedicated " or a single-track woman ; she had a profession for which she underwent a stiff training at an age when most of us would have hoped to have been rid of classes and examinations ; and she followed it with success. But she also had considerable organizing ability ; she was fully as successful as Dean of the School of Medicine as she was as a doctor, and she was remarkably good at running causes and getting subscriptions out of people. And she was happily married, the mother of two children ; and she ran in addition a full and vigorous social life, entertaining, giving parties, and generally meeting people of interest at the time. In fact, she was one of the first women to prove that a woman could have a successful career and be at the same time an all-round human creature. No doubt her vigorous health and tough, cheerful disposition helped her in this, but for those who were to come after it was as well to have it displayed.

LAURA KNIGHT

VI

LAURA KNIGHT

THE life of a painter has always been one which has attracted the imagination of many young persons. Leaving out actors and possibly now film-stars, I fancy that more novels and stories have been written about artists than about the members of any other profession, and that more young creatures have day-dreamed about taking up Art as a career and of painting the picture of the year in the Royal Academy (or any other important exhibition) than of any other career. Of course, it is always full-dress pictures which these aspirants want to paint ; by " artist " they mean somebody who has a great big studio and paints portraits or landscapes or what not ; they are not thinking of the comparatively humble craftsmen who merely design advertisements or illustrate Christmas catalogues or draw strip cartoons for cheap magazines. They are thinking of big pictures, for which you employ models and use a lot of paint, which are hung in exhibitions and eventually sold for enormous sums to millionaires or national art galleries.

But here there is a very great difference between genuine painters and dilettantes. Of course, there are in every generation just a few—not nearly so many as people sometimes think—of really great artists who are not recognized by their own contemporaries, and who, therefore, pass their lives in comparative obscurity and poverty, only to have their merits recognized long after they are dead. Such an artist was William Blake, of whose drawings nobody thought anything during his lifetime ; but they, as I have said, are very few, and their numbers are exceeded by those who were so fashionable when they lived that their pictures were bought by rich people for much more than they were worth—so that the buyers, or more often the buyers' children, found that thirty years later the pictures for which so much had been paid would fetch very little. Unrecognized geniuses apart, however, there is still a great gulf between serious painters and those who just play about with colours. Anna Zinkeisen, herself a distinguished designer and artist, has written rather trenchantly of the kind of " studio-lizard " who is to be found in great numbers in Chelsea and Bloomsbury.

"A studio all to herself," she says, " (deliciously artistic and important-sounding word ' studio '), no fixed hours for work or anything else, nothing to be done to order, and the most perfect freedom for self-expression in fancy overalls and all the privileged Bohemian stage-effects ; and, of course, a marvellous picture to be painted every now and then with a fine fury whenever the inspiration presents itself ; well, what in the world could be more delightful under the name of a career ? . . . The only serious drawback is that they seldom make any progress towards earning a living . . . though, *for those who are able to afford the luxury*, the life of an ineffective artist can be one of the happiest modes of existence. Bad artists swarm and thrive in all the most picturesque villages."

Laura Knight does not belong to this class, nor ever could have belonged to it, were she a much worse artist than she is. She is now at the top of the tree, can paint what she likes and command what prices she likes ; but she has only reached that position by intensely hard work, by determination to be a painter at all costs, and through poverty and hardship that would have daunted a good many people of less tough fibre and with less faith in themselves. Traces of the struggle exist, perhaps in the very hard and definite lines which are to be seen in much of her work—or perhaps this hardness is merely a reflection of her own vigorous temperament. However that may be, let any one who thinks that it is an easy job to become a famous artist read and ponder the life history of Laura Knight.

Born a contemporary of Mary Macarthur, she lived her early life in a blue slated semi-detached house in the old city of Nottingham. Unlike the majority of the distinguished women of whom I am writing, her childhood was not sheltered or protected, or her education given great thought or care. Anything less like the childhood of Lady Henry Somerset or of Clare Sheridan can scarcely be imagined. There were three Johnson sisters, Nellie, Sissie, and Laura, of whom Laura was the youngest. Their mother was Charlotte Johnson, herself an artist and teacher of art, whose chief delight it was to discover that her youngest daughter was born to be a painter, and that she was never so happy as with a pencil and paper in her hands. " Before I could speak or walk," she says, " I drew."

Her father had died when she was a baby, and Mrs. Johnson came back to live in her old home, where were also living grandmother, who was head of the household and perfectly capable of doing all the housework whether the family was well-off or ill-off, great-grandmother, who was over ninety and had to come down the stairs backwards, clinging to the banisters, and Uncle Arthur, who worked at the family lace business in Nottingham and frequently crossed to France to do business with another family lace-firm, run by a great-uncle and aunt of the young Johnsons, in St. Quentin.

From the very beginning Laura Johnson knew hardship ; at least, she knew monetary difficulties and the state of family affairs in which you could never be sure whether anything could or could not be afforded, whether you were going to be educated, have any toys or holidays, or get into debt. Most middle-class children are " sheltered " from these problems ; if their elders have financial troubles they are not discussed in front of the children, who only have to wonder whether their pocket-money will hold out, or to be annoyed to hear that they cannot go to the seaside this year. The young Johnsons were not sheltered ; they took part in the family troubles very early in life and were never able to feel irresponsible. If you have the stuff in you to stand it, this may well be a better education than the other kind.

Mrs. Johnson, after her husband's death, had been left practically penniless, and the family lace business, which was going downhill, could not afford to support her and her children. She got their education free, in exchange for teaching drawing and painting at Brincliffe School. When she was not in school she held private classes, where she taught sheltered young ladies to paint flowers on stools, fire-screens, fans, etc.—a horrible pursuit; she also kept up her own studies, and " when she had time " (!) painted pictures and tried to sell them. But it was a hard life, and grew steadily harder as the lace trade declined and the total income of the family in Noel Street declined with it. There was no money for holidays ; Laura never saw the sea until she was nine years old. There was no money for clothes ; Nellie's dresses were handed down through the family until they hung round little Laura's ankles, to her inconvenience and shame. Domestic help was reduced until Laura was the chamber-maid, and there was sometimes no money even for tram fares.

Nevertheless it was not an unhappy life. They were strong and vigorous children. Laura, who had always wanted to be a boy, was the strongest and the most excitable and boisterous ; and Nottingham was an interesting town for vigorous young things. Nowadays, Nottingham, to the ordinary spectator, looks much like any other big town ; but it has had a history. During the nineteenth century it had the reputation of being wild and lawless ; during the agitation for the great Reform Bill the people of Nottingham rioted in favour of it and burnt down Nottingham Castle ; in the generation before Laura it was full of young toughs with too little education and too much money to spend ; and the traditions still remained in the great excitements of Nottingham Goose Fair and Nottingham Races. The Johnsons' top windows overhung the race-course, and it is very probable that early memories of the Fair and the Races, which Laura Knight has so vigorously described in her book *Oil Paint and Grease Paint*, account in part for her eager painting of stage and circus in later life.

At twelve years old she was sent to her great-uncle and aunt in St. Quentin in northern France. They had offered to educate her free, with a view to letting her study at a Paris *atelier* later on. Of course, the intention was that she should earn her living as quickly as possible by her art ; her two elder sisters were already training to be Board School teachers—gloomy fate at the time. But Laura must have some general education as well,

DAME LAURA KNIGHT.

her mother said, though it is true that she did not get much, partly because her education was abruptly cut short, but partly, also, because she could not be got to take any interest in it. Her mother, who was never idle, told her that she would grow up an uneducated boor—readers of her books and admirers of her pictures will judge whether or not this prophecy has been fulfilled.

Laura's year in France was very different from the experience of those better-off young ladies who were at that time going to fashionable schools in Paris and Brussels in order to be " finished " for the marriage-market. The school itself, at which she slept in a long bare dormitory and worked at special art classes in the afternoon, she did not like for a long time, until she got used to it. She was, as always, short of money ; her clothes were made fun of by the French children, and she was regarded as naughty, and, worse than that, as immodest, because in the morning she stripped herself to the waist to wash, instead of dressing herself inside her night-gown and giving her face a rub with a sponge. Nevertheless, she notes, the French girls managed to look extraordinarily fresh and clean in spite of these scanty ablutions. It is a fact which has often puzzled Britons.

Even at that time she was buoyed up and kept from suicidal feelings by the thought that she could draw better than any of the other girls ; and during her time in France she was not by any means merely a schoolgirl. She was living in a French household, one which was intimately connected with a factory. There was only a door between the two, and when strikes or trouble threatened her great-aunt, a formidable woman, kept hold of a loaded pistol wherewith to cow anybody who tried to break in. She learnt how unsafe the streets of a French town were then for an unprotected girl, even so young a girl ; but she also learnt how deeply the French, whether Parisian or provincial, respect art and literature and the intellectual life. " It seemed that even to the meanest Frenchman an artistic talent was something to be revered." How different from England, then or now.

At the end of her first year the serious illness of her grandmother brought Laura back to England. Her mother met her with grief, though her grandmother was out of danger. For the eldest sister, Nellie, had been attacked even before Laura went away by an epidemic of influenza which was nearly as devastating as the one which raged through England immediately after the European War, and which actually killed more well-known people, ranging from the elder brother of George V. downwards. When they parted Nellie said to her sister, " I shall never see you again." Every one thought this was delirium, but within a little while Nellie was dead— as much of overwork in teaching and training to teach as of the influenza itself. Not only that, but there had been another failure of fortune. The family was selling up its house and going to live in a tiny one.

That year Laura, aged thirteen, enrolled as an

" artisan student "—so that she should not have to pay big fees—at the Nottingham School of Art. She was asked to give the profession she was intending to follow, and wrote down the word " Teatcher "—not a teacher of spelling, one hopes ! As her mother was well known as a teacher and artist, she was allowed to go straight into the Life Class, where they drew directly from living models, and not from plaster casts—a form of copying which has always driven her crazy. She was, however, only allowed to draw heads and clothed bodies ; even in 1893, it was still as shocking, in provincial towns at any rate, for girls and women to want to draw naked bodies as it had been for Elizabeth Garrett to want to dissect them in 1860. Nor was there much other artistic study possible. Nowadays, when good reproductions of all the great pictures can be bought in all sizes for a few pence or a few shillings, and when travelling exhibitions move around from town to town, it is difficult to realize how hard it was then for some one without money even to get a look at a good picture. Once her mother had taken Sissie and herself up for a cheap workmen's excursion to London to see the Academy ; when they returned they were so exhausted that they slept for two days ! Almost the only original art available in Nottingham was contained in old bound copies of *Punch*.

Nevertheless, Laura enjoyed immensely her first year at the Art School. She drew and drew, working as hard as she possibly could, and that not without criticism.

Some of the instructors thought her work so unfeminine and unladylike—" with those great thick lines," they said. " Why do you try to draw like a man ? Why can't you draw from your wrist, not from your shoulders?" She tried, or so she tells us, but without effect ; her drawings persisted in being unrefined, and she had, in spite of criticisms, the interest and encouragement of the school's star pupil, a dark-haired Nottingham lad, a few years older than herself, named Harold Knight. With him and with others she put in long hours of extra study, painting one another out of hours in the week-ends. Meantime her uncle had started a new small business which promised well, her mother was getting new pupils, and her grandmother, aged seventy-nine, doing all the work of the house with a little help from a small daily girl. They could not often afford meat, but they were doing a little better.

Disaster, however, was in store. The very next summer Mrs. Johnson, while away with some pupils on a holiday, fell down and broke her leg. She was ill for some time, during which Sissie, the elder sister, broke down and had to be sent away ; and soon afterwards she died.

This was a terrible time for a girl of fourteen. They could not possibly live without Mrs. Johnson's earnings, let alone afford anything for comforts for her—they could not afford a nurse at all—so Laura had to cut down her work at the Art School and try and take over her

mother's teaching and classes. Every one was anxious
to give her a chance, as they were all sorry for Mrs.
Johnson ; and fortunately she was already so excellent
a draughtsman—better, indeed, than her mother—that
there was no criticism of her on that score. But how
many girls of fourteen would like to take on the job
of visiting big houses to give lessons in painting, holding
classes of young ladies in their own homes, and, worst of
all, teaching art to classes of young girls, some of them
much older, in their own former school ? Most girls of
fourteen, I should think, would run away from it altogether ; but Laura Johnson was of tougher material
and, of course, owing to her upbringing, a good deal
advanced for her age. In fact, it was during that summer
that she and Harold Knight came to some sort of an
understanding, though there was no formal engagement ;
but the consciousness of it, I believe, helped to comfort
her mother on her death-bed. Not long after her mother's
death, her grandmother also died, and she and Sissie
were left alone in the world, at fifteen and seventeen,
orphans and practically penniless.

Then began perhaps the stiffest time of all, for Sissie
could not get work as a teacher, her health not being
strong enough, and the lessons which Laura gave, after
the first brave start, began to fall away. (Possibly the
early success was due to her mother's personality as much
as to her own ; a good artist need not be a good teacher,
and it would certainly have been unfortunate if Laura

Knight had settled down to be a teacher of art.) She kept such pupils as she could, charging five shillings a lesson, got a class of Board Schools teachers to train for ten pounds a year, and kept continually sending drawings to publishers and for competitions, but without any success. Besides her earnings, she and her sister were given five pounds a month by her uncle in France. Half of that went on rent and a lot more on gas and coal. They had no money for clothes (for some time they had one winter coat between them) and hardly any for food. For a long time, she says in her autobiography, they lived on porridge and bread and butter, until their throats struck work and refused to swallow the porridge until they had spent a week or two on a better diet. Paint and canvases could only be bought at great sacrifice ; models could not be paid for ; paintings and drawings would be sold in Nottingham market for anything they could fetch. (There are people in the world now who have bought an early Knight for a penny or twopence off the cobblestones.) Seldom can any painter have had so tough a start in life.

Still, one does not get the impression that everything was unrelieved gloom. They were young and full of spirits in spite of their diet. They had Harold Knight, then also a struggling painter, for companion ; and he and Laura painted and painted and talked to one another about what they would do. Laura won a gold medal at South Kensington and the Princess of Wales's scholarship for twenty pounds a year ; the medal she despised and sold for five pounds, but the scholarship came in useful. Harold won a fifty-pound travelling scholarship, and they both decided to leave the Art School, where they felt they had reached a dead end and were doing no good. Gradually Laura began to get one or two commissions to paint portraits at two, three, and five pounds a time ; and at length there came what almost appeared to be a visit from a fairy godmother. Her aunt from France arrived on an unexpected visit, found her nieces with nothing but tea and bread in the house, and, her French-trained soul absolutely horror-stricken, she insisted on stocking the larder with decent food and then sending them immediately away on a holiday. They went to a fishing village called Staithes on the north coast of Yorkshire, and from that time, it seems to me, dates Laura Knight's real growth as a painter, though there were still years to come before she made any money to speak of or even got any real recognition.

But in this tough, hard little village, houses jumbled right on top of one another in a steep cleft of the cliffs, as they are at Robin Hood's Bay, swept by fierce winds which were icy cold in winter, and inhabited by people who got all their hard living from the sea and never knew when the sea would exact their lives as the price of it, people with unmistakeable characters and unmistakeable faces, not like the limp dull rows whom one sees facing one in a Tube, Laura Johnson found both the

energy and the inspiration she needed. Battling with
gales on a Yorkshire coast, with good Yorkshire food
inside her, was very different from battling with sleet
and snow in a Nottingham street on a diet of porridge.
She felt grand, and ready to take any sort of part in the
life of the fisherfolk—helping the boats home in a gale,
baiting hooks, gutting fish, etc., though sometimes she
and her friends were made to feel how little they, with all
their health and strength, could really stand up to the
work which the fisher-girls did. For example, it was
one of the women's job to carry the wet fishing-nets in
skips or baskets on their heads, up to the top of the cliffs,
so that they could dry on the grass. One day Laura and
a friend, standing at the bottom, saw two old sisters,
both over eighty, waiting for the men to come and lift
the nets on their heads. The girls, thinking it a shame that
two poor old creatures should have to attempt this hard
job, offered to take their places ; but when the nets
were put on their heads, they were rooted to the ground !
They could not have taken a step on the level, far less
moved uphill. So they gave up their attempt to do a
Good Deed ; the old ladies resumed their nets, and
walked up the hill, " cackling with laughter." On
another occasion they found that the fishermen, tired of
rescuing them and their boat from difficulties with the
breakers, had managed to jam it behind their row of
cobles so that it could not be got down to the water.

There was a cottage to let on the hillside behind

Staithes, and Laura and her sister took it and moved in, hoping optimistically to live by the sale of sketches and possibly by taking pupils. After a while they gave up the connection with Nottingham altogether, and the pictures which filled the studio there and were not wanted in Yorkshire went to auction, where they fetched less than a penny each. Some years afterwards, Laura found two of them hanging on the walls of a house in Nottingham, and signed with a name which at the time was more distinguished than that of Laura Johnson. The owner refused to believe that they were in fact Laura Johnson's pictures : I do not know whether in later years he has seen occasion to alter his opinion.

For some years Laura and her sister lived in Yorkshire, either at Staithes or at Roxby on the moors. Alas ! I have no room, in the short space of a chapter, to tell anything like the full story of that Yorkshire life. Those who want more of it—and exciting and interesting it is, enough to make any girl want to leave a stuffy job and go to the northern moors to paint—must look for it in the fascinating first chapters of *Oil Paint and Grease Paint*. It was healthy, it was inspiring, and it was grand ; but it was still not at all remunerative. The big open air scenes and subjects needed more technique than Laura possessed to deal with them properly ; the sketches and studies would not come right. Pupils and commissions were rare ; all too typical was the Congregational minister who offered ten shillings for a water-colour of the rostrum in his chapel, but, though he liked the picture, did not pay the ten shillings. Laura's first genuine commission came through a man who had been offered it but did not want to do it himself. He described it to her— " A design for a show-card. A bloody sun must be shining on a bloody sea, on which these letters are to lie in perspective. ' The Sun Never Sets on Hawkes's Band Instruments.' " " I tried for three weeks," Laura writes, " to make a design from this motif that had artistic merit. Then, throwing Art to the winds, I did exactly what they wanted to their complete satisfaction. I needed that three guineas." Nevertheless she was learning all the time, the sort of thing which the layman, or one who simply stares at pictures never thinks of, but which artists have to learn in an almost intellectual manner, as economists have to learn the use of graphs and slide-rules—how to balance one colour with another, how to use red, say, so that the spectator's eye shall see green for itself near by, without a spot of green having been put on the canvas, and so on ; fascinating games and tricks to play, and invaluable for later work, when you want to have every trick at your fingers' ends and to get any effect you want without having to try and try. And in 1903 the tide began to turn. A letter came from London : it contained a varnishing ticket for a picture to be hung in the Royal Academy.

Laura was at that moment in a village in Nottingham-shire, having come there to be near Harold Knight, who, as the elder, had made further progress with his career and had got some commissions in Nottingham. They had decided to get married, though they had no immediate hopes of fortune ; and, having no money for railway fares or hotel bills, Laura did not go to London to see her first picture in the Academy. She stayed in the country trying to paint farm landscapes, but found the flat, wet country very dull after Yorkshire. A few days later came another letter from the Royal Academy, which said, " Your picture, *Mother and Child*, has been purchased by Edward Stott, R.A., for the sum of twenty pounds." She could not believe it at first ; she thought there must be some mistake, he could not have wanted the picture, he must have liked the frame—but the frame was not worth twenty pounds. However, there was no mistake : it was a good send-off for the wedding.

Laura and Harold Knight were not intending to set up an establishment together ; they were not interested in housekeeping but in painting, and they simply meant to live together wherever they could best get on with their work. Laura's wedding-dress was made by herself from a linen sheet which had formed part of her mother's trousseau. Their friends, knowing their intentions, gave them trunks, writing-cases, hat boxes—anything that could be used for packing up and moving on. After a short honeymoon, they came back to Yorkshire, to the cottage of a Mrs. Bowman at Roxby, where they painted and endeavoured to sell their work—the last a far harder task than the first. Laura has left a vivid description of trying to "interest" London picture-dealers in their work on an icy January day, hawking round bales of pictures and sketches which looked so imposing when they were packed up, but which the dealer handled with a sniff, as though they had been a pack of dirty playing-cards—and then showed them abominations which he declared were really good stuff, and in the public taste. At least, writers who send unwanted books to publishers do not have to watch the publishers' faces when they read them. After this expedition they returned to Roxby, where they lived for some time on credit granted by their landlady, having put aside just enough to pay for the packing and carriage of their pictures to next year's Academy. In case the pictures should be hung, they wrote to an old friend of Harold's asking for a loan of five pounds to enable them to go up to London and see them, and meantime darned, patched, sponged, and pressed their clothes so as to have just one tolerably presentable suit each. On the Saturday before varnishing day, the post brought three letters : one enclosed five pounds, the others were from the Royal Academy, notifying them both that their pictures were hung. They decided to go to London by a cheap Easter Sunday excursion train from Whitby. This meant a walk of thirteen miles across the moor, most of which was performed in drenching rain. They came into York station restaurant so wet that when they approached near the fire they filled the room with steam ; they arrived at King's Cross at four in the morning to find all the waiting-rooms full. Still in their wet clothes, for they had no others, they went to Burlington House a few hours later, to be met by a friend who told them that Harold's picture was hung " on the line "—the best position in the Academy—and had been bought for a hundred pounds by Frank Dicksee for the Brisbane Art Gallery. It all reads like a fairy tale.

Five days later they returned home, with a shilling between them and a cold apiece, caught in the warm air of London. But they had a hundred pounds in prospect, and they had arranged to hold an exhibition at the Leicester Galleries. They were now fairly launched.

For the next few years Laura Knight's life is of less interest to the general reader—more like the life of many another artist of less than her powers. The most important thing about it, for her, seems to have been that for the first time since those hard early days at the Nottingham Art School—which perhaps scarcely counted—she began to be regularly meeting and working and discussing with other artists, a thing which every painter ought to do from time to time, if he knows how to benefit by criticism and other people's experiences. Laura Knight is a thoroughly individual painter ; her own style is un-mistakeable, but she would be the first to own how much she has learnt from study both of old masters and of contemporaries. From now on, her reminiscences become fuller and fuller of the names of other artists—painters, of course, primarily, but also musicians, singers, dancers, authors, and eventually, though not until later, actors, acrobats, and circus people.

With other artists they spent months at a time in Holland, that haunt of artists both living and dead. They stayed first at a *pension* in Laren full of painters, called the Pension Karn from the name of the proprietress, and afterwards moved on to farms in the neighbourhood. It was the regular thing to hire a resting-place in one of the farms, some of which had huge lighted barns as big as any studio, and for five gulden a week you had the right to roam wherever you liked, set up your easel in any room, even the kitchen or a bedroom with somebody in bed, and use as models any member of the household who had time to pose. The peasants were used to artists wandering about, and took no more notice of them than if a pig had strayed in—in fact, the artists were sometimes more incommoded by the smell of the goats and pigs which " lived in " on the smaller farms than the peasants were by the artists. In the intervals of painting they went by tram or train to the big towns, to stare and stare at the collections of Rembrandts and other masterpieces in the galleries, and had long discussions about the principles and practice of art.

For three years the Knights went at intervals to Holland, staying months at a time, learning, and painting pictures whose sale paid for their next trip. When they came back for the last time to England, after a bitterly hard winter, they found that they no longer had any desire to live in Yorkshire. It was cold and hard ; it was dark and bleak for painting, and the lives of its people were full of tragedy. They missed, besides, the happy companionship of painters that they had had in Holland. After some heart-searching, during which Laura felt almost like a traitor to the people she had known so long, who had helped her in the days of discouragement to gain strength and to find out what she might do, in November 1907 they decided to join their fellow-artists in Cornwall—which had for many years been a haunt of painters. They settled in Newlyn, where Laura found a large studio. The previous tenant, she notes, must have been very rich, because where she cleaned her palette she had wiped off immense masses of unused paint on the beams, which could all be used again. " I did not buy expensive colours such as cadmium for over a year." Nevertheless, the time was now very near when Laura Knight would not care two hoots how much cadmium she bought.

The change came quickly, almost abruptly ; and it is an extraordinary thing how often, in the life-history of artists, there is a great jump, it seems, from comparative poverty to comparative affluence—splendid for the artist, if he or she can only " stick out " the early days. Laura Knight had certainly done some sticking out ; after a brilliant early start, when she looked as though she might turn out an infant prodigy, she had struggled for years with poverty and complete lack of recognition. She certainly deserved anything she might get.

Nevertheless, it was an astonishingly rapid change. For the first years of their married life the Knights, though " rising " young painters, were certainly not well off ; they had to go to Holland by the cheapest possible route, and at least once they were down to their last few shillings when a buyer of pictures turned up. Not that they minded that much : they never worried deeply about lack of cash, and even in later years they more than once found that they were completely cleaned out. But in later years impecuniosity was not due to low prices paid for pictures.

In 1906 or thereabouts Laura writes that " Mr. Hayward came; he bought four of Harold's pictures and three of mine. The cheque came to nearly a hundred pounds "—an average of £14 a picture, which is certainly not dear. But in 1910 or 1911, of a big picture called *Daughters of the Sun*, one of the first big pictures which she did in Cornwall, she writes again : " It was exhibited at the Royal Academy, the effect [of a new technique for painting sunlight] extraordinarily glowing. On its account I had there a *succès d'estime*, but not financially ; I received an offer of *three hundred pounds* for it—to accept so great a reduction of the original price would have been an indignity." In 1912 also the picture called *The Green Feather*—of which more hereafter—was sold to the National Gallery of Ottawa for £400. This is not any longer the work of a struggling painter—in four or five years a " Laura Knight " had become a real piece of property, a thing which dealers were eager to buy, feeling sure that they would be able to sell it to the public. And when dealers start to have confidence in a painter, that painter's prices go up by leaps and bounds.

The tale of *The Green Feather* must be told, for it is so typical, both of the painter and her painting. Laura Knight had an emerald green dress, of stiff silk, with a tight bodice and a wide flowing skirt, and she decided that she would paint a big outdoor picture of her friend Dolly Snell wearing it. It was October when the canvas, $7\frac{1}{2}$ feet by 5, arrived, and the beautiful autumn weather might break at any moment. So having prepared the canvas overnight with oil and turps, she started work at eight the following morning, intending at the time only " to do the most work possible on the first day." The wooden stretcher of the canvas was fixed on six poles ; but in the night the wind had become fresh, and nothing on earth would prevent the canvas from bellying in and out. All the drawing and modelling had to be done with the palette shoved hard against the cloth to keep it momentarily steady.

This for a start. For additional difficulty, Nature played one of the tricks which she keeps up her sleeve for painters. The day had started solid grey, though a sunlit picture had been the intention ; so solid grey it was painted. But about one o'clock, when painter and sitter had stopped for a hasty bite of bread and cheese, the clouds rolled away, brilliant blue sky and sunshine appeared—and stayed. Most of the picture had to be painted over again, as of course all the colours were different. Nevertheless, everything went so well, and the painter, stimulated by hourly drinks of black coffee, painted with such vigour and accuracy that by half-past five, when she stopped to gather up the brushes which she had thrown down in dozens all over the field, and to clean the paint off her hair, there was only half an hour's work remaining to be done—which was successfully completed next morning before the rain fell in torrents. Of course, this is not the usual way in which a picture, even a picture by Laura Knight, proceeds ; it was a magnificent *tour de force*. Big pictures are more often preceded by weeks of sketching, making studies and designs, and having a succession of shots which do not come off. The point is that this day's work, sold, as I have said, for four hundred pounds, could not have been done by any one who did not possess Laura Knight's superb energy and stamina or her mastery of line and colour, the technique of her job.

When an artist, or indeed almost any one in any profession, has reached real success, the further history of her life is of rather less interest to ordinary people, particularly young people, unless, indeed, she changes her whole walk of life, as did Annie Besant, and gains mastery in something new. From the painting of *The*

Green Feather Laura Knight has gone on from strength to strength and from honour to honour. She was asked during the war to paint for the Canadian War Expeditionary Force ; she went to the United States on an extremely successful tour ; she has received any number of commissions and had her pictures bought by many national and municipal galleries, including the Tate Gallery ; in 1927 she was elected an Associate of the Royal Academy, being the second woman to be so honoured since 1769 ; in 1931 the University of St. Andrews gave her the honorary degree of Doctor of Law. (The unsophisticated may find it comic that such a degree should be conferred upon Laura Knight, who on her own showing had practically no formal education and probably knows less about law than you or I do ; but it is only the odd way universities have of showing that they think certain persons are public figures of importance. The granting of this degree meant that Laura Knight was not merely a brilliant painter, but a national personage.) But in my feeling the chief interest of the last twenty years is the switching over of her mind and gifts to the subjects which captured her imagination in childhood—fair and circus life.

She came to it, so it would seem, partly by way of stage and ballet. Dolly Snell, the Green Feather model, was a dancer, and Laura Knight, before the war, went to ballet classes with her. Before the war, also, she first saw Anna Pavlova, whom many people think the best

dancer who ever appeared on any stage, and was immediately fascinated. " Pavlova," she says, " had the
perfect body for her art " ; and she drew and painted
her over and over again from every possible angle.
Once, even, Pavlova posed for her standing on the point
of one toe with her leg stretched straight out, for five whole
minutes—no small feat, either for the artist who held that
position, or for the other artist who in five minutes
finished the drawing. But while watching and drawing
Pavlova she also watched and drew the stage surroundings
in which she danced, and gathered an almost wild
inspiration from the effects which she saw—the reflections
of the stage lights on the furnishings of the auditorium, the
picking out of bits of colour, shine and shadow in the
clothes and faces of the audience, and, most fascinating
of all, the " backstage " scenes, the big dressing-room of
the *corps de ballet*, with its stone steps, its flaring lights and
cracked mirrors and the girls with beautiful bodies in
every stage of dress and undress. After Pavlova she
worked and painted on stage and off in many productions, in *The Annunciation*, in *Romeo and Juliet*, and
above all in the great Diaghilev Russian Ballet that took
London by storm immediately after the war. After that
she turned to the circus. She painted at Olympia, which
must have been exciting enough ; but she was not
content with a stationary circus. She followed Carmo's
Circus round the roads, from Chatham to Margate, to
Folkestone, and right to Blackpool, painting and drawing

all the way. And not merely painting or learning to paint—as she says, " I think I can paint any horse now," though she had never really come into contact with horses till the circus days—but living in and with the circus, frying the bacon and eggs for breakfast, helping serve and wash up the refreshments, nearly getting walked on by the elephant, or pinned in a corner against the rump of a zebra, thinking and breathing circus. There is no room here to retell her own stories of circus life—those who, like myself, are sorry that this is so, will find plenty of them in *Oil Paint and Grease Paint*. But the remarks with which she ends her chapters on the circus may serve well for an epilogue to this chapter, and may also explain what it is which, added to her natural gifts, make of Laura Knight a painter whose strength and vitality make every-thing she does, whether her composition—which is, on the whole, her weak point—is good or not, stand right out from the work of most painters.

" Harold said, ' You are mad—circus-crazy.' So I was. . . . It was just the same with the ballet, he said.

" When with fisher-people, the theatre, the circus, or any other grade of society, I cannot withhold the vital interest that burns inside for the work they themselves do and what it means to them if they are sincere.

" Painting, music, ballet, theatre, circus, art, and physical skill, what joy to project oneself in each, to feel the daring of the acrobat, the control of the artist, in understanding and sympathy to live many lives in one."

189

ANNIE BESANT

VII

ANNIE BESANT

IT is always risky, and sometimes dangerous, to make comparisons between people. But I feel there is no great risk in saying that, of all the women who appear in this book, Annie Besant was, *as a personality*, the most remarkable. She was, in fact, a saint.

Many people who knew Annie Besant will be astonished to see that word used, and will ask whether I really mean that Annie Besant was a compound of all the copybook virtues, or that I should advise small girls to set her life before them as a pattern. I should not, certainly ; but I do mean that if Annie Besant had lived in another period of history, say, the Middle Ages, and had been, as she then would have been, a faithful child of the Church, she would almost certainly by now have been canonized, and be called Saint Anne. People who find this hard to believe have forgotten that the word " saint " is used in two senses. The first kind of saint is the one who keeps all the rules, who is meek, pious, humble, and obliging—what we are apt to mean, in fact, when we say to some one, " Oh, do be a saint and darn my stockings for me." The other is quite an opposite type—a person of enormous dynamic force and intense conviction, often amounting to a feeling of absolute inspiration, which breaks through all bonds and all precedents and alters the course and shape of things around them. This kind of saint arouses violent enthusiasm and also violent antagonisms : because they are so convinced of their own right inspiration, and because they are human as well, they make the most colossal mistakes at times. They may appear to be monsters, because they do not allow the ties and emotions which bind ordinary people to stand in the way of what they believe to be right ; but they have, at the same time, that tremendous driving power which moves mountains which seemed absolutely immovable, and which infects other, more ordinary people with force which they did not know they possessed and enables them to remove lesser mountains of their own. They may create tremendous controversy, and make people exceedingly angry ; but at long last, when all the shouting has died down, there will be no doubt in the minds of the majority who have met them that they have been in contact with something quite out of the ordinary, something which makes their whole lives seem different. Such a saint, as anybody who troubles to read real history can easily find out, was St. Theresa or Joan of Arc ; and of such was Annie Besant. (We shall see later how closely she resembled the saints of history in certain respects, such as her tendency towards mysticism and her impatience of family ties.) If, as I said, she had lived five hundred years ago, she would by now have been canonized, and her life carefully edited in small books for children to read. But she died only a year or two ago ; and accordingly she is not a canonized saint, only a woman whom some people despised and execrated and thousands of others regarded with passionate adoration.

Annie Besant had a long life, from 1847 to 1933. As she had also practically unbounded physical and mental energy—for example, she wrote four or five hundred books and pamphlets and an infinite quantity of articles ; and when over sixty she learnt to drive her own car, and at seventy-nine did an aeroplane propaganda tour over Europe—she embarked upon all sorts of activities and promoted all sorts of causes. It is impossible, in a chapter, to do more than mention some of the most interesting ; but it is worth remembering that, whatever she did, she did with all her force, and that her force was equal to that of several ordinary people. A cause which gained Annie Besant's support felt as if it had enlisted an army with banners.

She was born in London, the second child of William Persse Wood and his wife, who had been Emily Morris. A brother, Henry, two years older, was the only other child to survive. Her parents were not commonplace people. Her father, Dr. Wood, though he came of a highly respectable middle-class family, was a strong sceptic, a disbeliever in revealed religion of any kind ; whereas her mother was a mystic of the Irish kind, who had second-sight, believed in banshees and ghosts, and showed many signs of that queer unexplained sensitiveness which some people possess and which we call telepathy. Her husband laughed at her, and like a good Victorian wife she put up with it, though, as will appear, she had plenty of character of her own.

When Annie was five years old, her father, who, though he had ceased to practise medicine, occasionally assisted in dissection, scratched his finger while performing a post-mortem on a man who had died of tuberculosis, and within a very few weeks was dead himself. One of Annie's earliest recollections was of sitting in a room with her mother and her aunts and grandmothers, all in black, when the hearse had left for the cemetery, her mother, white-faced and with watch in hand, following in telepathic imagination the progress of the coffin until with a shriek of " It's all over ! " she fell in a faint on the floor.

Dr. Wood's death left his family badly off ; but Mrs. Wood resisted all attempts to make them " come down in the world," and all kind offers to provide a City clerkship for little Henry. She was determined that her son should be brought up like a gentleman through school and university, and having discovered that the fees for Harrow were reduced for boys living in the town, she moved into lodgings there and after a while secured a house, where she took in other boys as boarders. Eventually, with the help of the headmaster, she became quite successful ; but her husband's relatives were so shocked at her independence and at her taking in boarders that they would not keep up relations with her, and actually they scarcely met again.

In that house—a rambling sort of place built high on Harrow Hill, covered with ivy and climbing roses, and looking over green fields to London far away—Annie spent the next two or three years of her life. She was an eager, lively, and cheerful child—they called her " Sunshine "—and passionately devoted to her mother, for whom her affection sometimes got to be an embarrassment. " If you will follow Mamma around like that, Annie," she said once, " I shall have to get a string and tie you to my apron, and how will you like that ? "

" Oh, Mamma darling," said Annie, " *do* let it be in a knot ! "

She had no small friends of her own, but played with her brother and his fellow pupils from the school, particularly at " boys' games "—cricket and tree-climbing, etc.—which was rather shocking for a little girl in the 'fifties. It does not seem as though she had any particular affection for her brother ; in her autobiography she explains, with rather naïve vanity, that she often beat him at boys' games. Perhaps she was slightly jealous of him for being a boy and unrestricted.

For the rest, she was an excitable child with a vivid imagination, who told herself stories and day-dreams in the intervals of play. She imagined herself leading hosts upon a charger, with white armour and tossing hair ; she loved to be with her Morris aunts, listening to tales about saints and ghosts in Ireland ; and while she was quite young she discovered how lovely is the *sound* of poetry. Milton caught this seven-year-old's fancy— rather heavy going, one might think, for her age, but poetry with a splendid rolling noise. She sat in the branches of an old apple tree declaiming to herself :

" Thrones, dominations, virtues, princes, powers,"

and also composing prayers which she rolled out in a voice as sonorous as she could make it.

This life soon came to an end. Mrs. Wood did not know how to arrange for Annie's education ; her own life at Harrow was dedicated to Henry's, and though we are not told so, it seems probable that Henry and his friends did not care particularly to have Annie tagging round after them and beating them at their games. So when she was eight years old she was sent to board at a school in Dorsetshire, kept by Miss Florence Marryat, sister of the Captain Marryat who wrote sea-stories. This parting from her mother was her first great shock. She could not have believed that her mother could really bear to let her go to school, and she never really forgave her brother for being, as she dimly felt, the cause of it.

Once the wrench was over, however, she was happy enough with Miss Marryat, who seems to have been a sensible and intelligent woman who tried to train her charges' minds, not merely to stuff them with information. The atmosphere of the school was religious, as indeed were all Victorian schools, but not religious enough for Annie ; for the religion taught was of the quiet, rather drab kind associated with Evangelicalism, and what Annie wanted was colour and passion and devotion. She wanted to be immensely excited, to worship something with her whole heart, to die a martyr or to die leading martyrs. If she had been brought up a Roman Catholic she would certainly have wanted to become a nun.

She stayed with Miss Marryat until she was sixteen, by which time her education was " finished " and she went home to Harrow. Not much is told us of her schooldays, but we know that Miss Marryat, in an attempt to broaden her charges' minds, took Annie and another girl called Emma Mann to Bonn on the Rhine and to Paris. The Bonn trip ended in disaster, for at the same hotel there were staying with a tutor the two sons of the Duke of Hamilton. They were amused at and interested in the girls ; they made faces at them. And Lord Charles, the younger, used to move his scalp and waggle his ears in a way that made these shocking young females —they were then thirteen and fourteen—dissolve in giggles. Miss Marryat, who for all her intelligence was a good deal of a fluttering spinster, instantly removed them to a girls' school, where German students, with cheeks gashed in duels, whispered compliments to them in the streets ! In Paris no such *contretemps* occurred, only Annie discovered the pomp of ritual and incense in the churches, and returned to England more passionately religious than ever.

When she was back at home this passion continued. She took no interest in social affairs, in her brother's friends, now grown-up, or in the young masters from Harrow who came to the house and were met at parties. Her mother, perhaps with a feeling that she had rather sacrificed her to Henry in childhood, did everything she could for her, made her clothes, did her hair, and dressed her in all her petticoats and laces for social gatherings ; but though Annie was happy in these attentions, it made little difference. She played croquet and the piano well, and that and her good looks made her generally acceptable ; but she was not interested in anything but religion. She moved among them, as her biographer says, " impersonal as a beautiful nun " ; and when some of the young men asked her to marry them, she was so little interested that she did not even mention it to her mother. Few would have guessed that the fastings and self-tortures through which she put herself, the church services and ecstasies through which she went, were the beatings of a daemonic energy which was crying out for some work to do. It got loose at last, but not before she

MRS. ANNIE BESANT.

had gone through an experience which, unpleasant as it was, was no more in fact than an incident in her life.

The Christmas when she was eighteen she spent with relations at Chelsea, including an aunt, nearly of her own age, who was a passionate ritualist, and adored very formal Church services, with a great deal of singing, fine robings, and elaborate prayers and ceremonies. It was the time of the Tractarian movement, led by men like Cardinal Newman and Dr. Pusey, who endeavoured, among other things, to make the ritual of the Church of England more like that of the Church of Rome. Taken by her Aunt Minnie to their church at Chelsea, she liked it so much that she returned there at Easter-time ; and then found that the vicar had a new curate, a young man from Cambridge named Frank Besant.

Frank Besant was an ordinary enough young fellow in reality, when you removed his surplice and took him out of the gloom of his half-lit church—a rather per-nickety, rather pedantic person with all the ordinary conventions. But Annie Wood never looked on the real man ; she thought of him as though he were always wearing his surplice, and was prepared to pour upon him all the admiring devotion she would have felt for a Prince of the Church. Frank Besant had no notion of all this. He only saw an attractive girl who listened to him with very flattering attention ; and he proposed to continue the good work by joining her family at St. Leonards-on-Sea during his summer holiday. After a

very pleasant week, during which Frank Besant and
Annie Wood, as the only two young people in the party,
spent a good deal of time together, Annie was staggered
to discover that Besant considered that she had practically
promised to be his wife.

She had not intended this. She was thinking of discussions on religion and of the glamour of the Church,
not of becoming anybody's wife. But in those days, if a
girl went about at all in the company of a young man,
there was always presumed to be "something" in it.
When Frank Besant formally asked Mrs. Wood if he
might marry her daughter, she was very unwilling to
give her consent. She thought they were ill-suited to one
another, and so they certainly were. But Annie, with a
curious blind obstinacy, felt that her mother was trying
to thwart her religious aspirations—Mrs. Wood had very
little sympathy with fastings and elaborate ceremonials
—and she insisted on getting married. Of Frank Besant's
tastes and character I really believe she had not the smallest idea. Throughout her long life, Mrs. Besant's judgment of people was never her strong point ; she was always
liable to invest persons with characteristics which they
did not possess. Saints are like that ; their intense con-
centration blinds them to what is happening around
them.

It was a brief and disastrous marriage, and it was
really nobody's fault. Frank Besant was not an imagina-
tive or generous man ; but he can hardly be blamed for

not being able to cope with the force to which he had linked himself. He wanted a nice quiet help-mate, who would keep his house, bear his children, darn his stockings, do such other duties as were suitable to his calling, and take her spiritual guidance from him. Instead he got an elemental creature full of unused energy, who was dismally bored by domesticity, and all the ladies with whom she was supposed to be acquainted, who had no nice flow of soothing small-talk, but an ardent desire to discuss the dogmas and truths of religion, and who, after a very few years, had argued herself into disbelief in nearly all the things which he had accepted, and could not attend to the housework because she was lying on her bed in mental and physical agony, wrestling with the doctrine of the Trinity or some problem of that sort. What an uncomfortable situation for a vicar !

As to Annie, she ought never to have been married except to some one who was her intellectual equal ; and it is at least doubtful whether she ought to have brought up children. She had two, a boy and a girl ; but, though she talked as though she was very devoted to the girl, at any rate, and nursed her almost passionately through an illness, her language suggests more that she was working up maternal feelings in herself because she felt she ought to have them, than that she really cared for her child above all else. Not all women are natural mothers, though some people write as though they ought to be ; and Mrs. Besant certainly had no taste for the life of an

English wife of the middle class Bitterly she wrote of the ladies of Cheltenham, where she lived after her marriage :

" Ladies who talked to me only about babies and servants,—*troubles of which I knew nothing and which bored me unutterably* [!]—and who were as uninterested in all that had filled my life, in theology, in politics, in science, as I was uninterested in the discussion on the housemaid's young man, and on the cook's extravagance in using butter, ' when dripping would have done perfectly well, **my** dear ! ' "

In her boredom she began for the first time to write. She wrote a short story for the *Family Herald*, a paper which used to be the favourite Sunday reading of the English middle classes. It was a bad, silly, sentimental story ; but at least she got thirty shillings for it, which made her feel just a little independent. She tried to write a serial, but the editor would have none of it, saying that it was " too political." So she took to writing pamphlets about religion.

The Besants were married at the end of 1867. By 1873 the marriage had come to an end. Annie had become more and more out of sympathy with her husband, more and more of a disbeliever in religion ; and he, after efforts to persuade her by reasonable means, reached the conclusion that she ought to be disciplined. He might as well have tried to discipline a whirlwind. There were humiliating quarrels, and in 1873 she fled to her mother in London, and announced that she would not return to her husband.

After some argument a separation was arranged. Mr. Besant agreed to allow his wife £110 a year, and the charge of the little girl, then three years old, the boy remaining with his father. Mrs. Besant immediately set to work to support herself and the small Mabel. She had a hard job in front of her, for, beside the fact that £110 was not much of an income for any one who had always lived comfortably, the dice were very much loaded, in the eighteen-seventies, against women who had left their husbands. It was generally assumed that they must be in the wrong.

She started out at once, by taking a job as children's governess in a family in return for board and lodging for herself and Mabel, intending to save up her allowance in order to furnish them a home. This first job proved no sinecure, for almost immediately the children fell ill of diphtheria and scarlet fever, and she nursed them throughout the winter. Immediately afterwards another blow fell on her. In the spring of 1874 she was summoned back to London to nurse her mother ; and after a long and exhausting illness Mrs. Wood died. As she lay on her death-bed, thinking sadly that she must leave her daughter at this very difficult time of her life, she murmured to her, " My little one, you have never made me sad or sorry except for your own sake ; you have always been too religious." And to herself, " Yes, that has been darling Annie's only fault ; she has always been too religious."

It was true, from Mrs. Wood's own point of view, even if it was not the whole truth. It had at any rate more truth in it than Annie's reproach to her mother for having damaged her life by keeping from her the truth about the world. For, as far as one can see, Mrs. Wood, as far as her knowledge went, always did tell Annie the truth about the world ; it was Annie who would not take it in. As regards her marriage, for example, it was Mrs. Wood who had the doubts, but it was absolutely impossible to convey them to Annie, with her head in the clouds. There are some people who are incapable of listening to argument until their minds have been prepared for it ; and Annie Besant was one of them.

The death of her mother shows again how really independent her mind was of family ties. She had, to all appearances, been devoted to her mother, and she had nursed her through a long illness. One would have expected her to be prostrated with grief. But, though she grieved, she was not prostrated ; and immediately began upon literary work, which she obtained through friends she had made in the course of her struggles about religion —friends, like Mr. Thomas Scott, who, without being atheists, had difficulties about some of the teachings of the Church. Mr. Scott set her to do writing for him and research in the British Museum ; and one day, in the course of her researches, she came across a copy of a periodical named *The National Reformer*, and in it found a notice of a body calling itself the National Secular Society. A few days later she went to a lecture in the Hall of Science at Hoxton, where the speaker was the leader of the Free-thinkers, Charles Bradlaugh.

It is difficult for us, unless we have a good deal of historical imagination, to re-create in our minds the state of things in which free-thought, *i.e.* the right to disbelieve openly in God and religion, could be a cause for which people would spend themselves to the last ounce, and which was as inspiring as any religion has ever been. Nowadays, we are inclined to feel that whether a man is religious or not is his own affair, and not to get very much excited about it. But, in those days, religion, and particularly the form of religion expressed in the Church of England, was still an engine of oppression. It was not so long since Roman Catholics had been denied the right of voting for Parliament ; and far less long since Charles Darwin's book, *The Origin of Species*, now accepted as one of the classics of biology, had been cursed by the Church because it seemed to conflict with something in the first book of the Bible. A very few years before Annie Besant's marriage, the Test and Corporation Acts were still in force, which forbade any one who was a Nonconformist, *i.e.* who belonged to any church except the Church of England, to be admitted to Oxford or Cambridge—and, of course, the position was much worse for any one who disbelieved in any church at all. The fact was, that the Church of England had for long been an upper-class association, patronized and run by respectable people, with no place in it for the poor unless they touched their caps and pulled their forelocks and did what their betters told them. The vicar was almost as much a power in the country village as the squire ; and a man whose religious views were unpleasing to him ran a good risk of losing his job, being turned out of his house, and even having to leave the place. Things were not quite so unfair in the towns ; but even there pressure was severe, as the early history of Charles Bradlaugh shows.

Bradlaugh came of much poorer people than Mrs. Besant. His mother was a nursemaid, and his father a clerk who served for twenty-two years at two pounds a week, for which he received no rise in wages, but a notice in the *Times* after his death commemorating his faithful service. Eldest of five children, Charles left school at twelve and went to work in the same office as his father. He was a boy of ability and intelligence, and soon was teaching other boys in Sunday-school. But as his studies went on he began to doubt some of the things he was taught, and when he asked a question of his vicar, the vicar, who cannot, one feels, have been very tactful, called him a young atheist, and turned him out of the Sunday-school. He was not an atheist then, but after the Sunday-school episode he soon became one, and started attending meetings where free-thought was discussed. The vicar took action again, and young Charles was told by his employers that he had three days in which to recant his opinions. He refused, and at sixteen was sacked and turned out upon the world. Nowadays it would seem to us extraordinary to deprive a lad of his job—unless it was a job in the Church—because he was not a Christian. But Bradlaugh never forgot it, never forgot this example of what happened to a poor man whose opinions failed to please his superiors, and the fight on which he then embarked merged in the general fight for freedom of opinion, freedom of speech, and freedom of the Press in this country—the fight which began with John Milton and his friends in the seventeenth century and has not been perfectly won to-day. And when I say fight, it was in Bradlaugh's case, if not an actual fight, a long and determined struggle. He would not submit, and he would not encourage others to submit to the sort of penalties which free-thought entailed. He spoke and wrote against them all his life ; he brought actions to the courts for wrongful dismissal and other suits. And, as the law is expensive, he pretty soon found that the money he could make by speaking—and he was a brilliant speaker—flowed away almost as fast as he could make it. It was the more unfortunate that he had married, in early life, a young woman who became a dipsomaniac, and whom he had to maintain in a home for many years, as well as bringing up his two daughters. No one knew anything about this until his wife was dead.

Meantime, he did not confine his battle for free speech to the courts. He became one of the best-known touring speakers of Victorian England. He spoke in many districts—in the east and north of London, in the mining villages, and in the great factory towns. Inevitably, it was to working-class audiences that he chiefly spoke, and it was the working men who called him " our Charlie " and loved and followed him as a leader. He founded and edited a journal, *The National Reformer*, and he stood for Parliament in the City of Nottingham, though it was not until 1880 that he was at last elected, after many contests, and not for another six years that Parliament would allow the man who had been chosen by the electors of Nottingham to take his seat.*

This was the man, tall and powerful, with a big head and a tremendous voice, whom Annie Besant met for the first time in a dingy hall in Hoxton in 1874. In after years, when she had become leader of the Theosophists and believed in reincarnation, she was wont to say that the fact that Bradlaugh went up to her immediately after the meeting and said, " Mrs. Besant ? " implied that they must have known one another before in a previous existence. No such explanation is really necessary. She had

---

* They refused him because as a free-thinker who did not believe in oaths, he could not take the oath of allegiance to the Queen, and asked to be allowed to " affirm," as many witnesses do in courts of law. Eventually, the matter was settled by a law being passed to allow M.P.'s to affirm. Bradlaugh then took his seat, but he was old and broken by his long fight, and died four years afterwards.

written to Bradlaugh before the meeting ; her name was known among people like Thomas Scott ; and it was un-usual, in the London of the 'seventies, for beautiful young women of twenty-six to attend meetings in East End halls. Bradlaugh would have been singularly slow in the uptake had he failed to guess who she was.

Be that as it may, from the moment at which he and Mrs. Besant met one another they recognized instantly that they had much to talk over and must see one another again. He gave her the certificate of membership of the National Secular Society, for which she had made previous application, and invited her to come and see him next day. Next day she came to his lodgings in White-chapel and was startled to see how drab and poor they were—representing a shabbiness which she had hardly known existed, for comparatively badly off as she was at the moment, she was adding to her hundred a year by some writing and research, and still more by selling jewels and expensive clothes which she now no longer needed. With no more, however, than a casual glance round, she began eagerly to talk to him. She poured out all she had been thinking and studying during the past two years about religion, and began to read to him parts of a pam-phlet which she was trying to write on *The Existence of God*. At one point in the reading Bradlaugh interrupted her. " Mrs. Besant," he said, " you have thought your-self into atheism without knowing it." When they parted she asked him to call on her.

He did not respond immediately. He warned her that if she took up with the Free-thinkers, she might well be committing social suicide. She had already sunk, in the estimation of "nice" people, by leaving her husband; but she was still associating with the respectable. If she joined Bradlaugh and his forces, she would be associating with outcasts, people who were accused of trying to break up the home and the State, people who got " moved on " and hustled by the police, and whose names made the respectable spit and splutter. He begged her to count the cost and to remember that all he could offer her in compensation was a guinea a week as a writer on the *National Reformer*. (Even that, though, represented a fifty per cent. rise in her income.) She was not moved by his warnings : I doubt whether she even listened to them. She had found the cause which she wanted—a cause which excited her passionate sincerity and which was altruistic rather than personal, and a cause, moreover, which was ready to use every bit of her energy which it could get. Within a month she had written her first article, under the pen-name of Ajax, for the *National Reformer*, and the night it went to press she made her first public speech, and thereby opened the way to triumphs of which she had never dreamed.

I have mentioned that Annie Wood, as a little girl, loved to declaim prayers and poetry. But there was no place in her life for little girls who could declaim, and it was only when she had been some time married that she heard her own voice again. In the middle of the quarrels with her husband, she one day rushed in despair to the church of Sibsey in Lincolnshire, where he was then vicar, and as she sat there, moodily wondering what was to become of her, an uncontrollable desire came upon her to go into the pulpit. She climbed up, and from there let her marvellous voice ring out around the church in an impassioned, impromptu sermon. She told nobody, and hurried home, rather ashamed and alarmed in case any one had heard so frightful a thing as the vicar's wife shouting from the vicar's pulpit. But now, in the bosom of the Secular Society, she found her voice again, and after a very few meetings became, as she continued to be for the rest of her life, the greatest woman orator in England. Her writing was apt to be dull and unremarkable, except when she was really indignant ; she wrote too much, and was always too busy to revise. But her oratory was perfect, and never failed of its object, even when she challenged terrific odds.

Her rise in the Society which she had joined was startling. Only a few weeks after their first meeting, Bradlaugh had to leave on a six months' tour of America. Before he went, he set Mrs. Besant on the path to become a national speaker, when he came back, he found her already so well-known as to be only second to himself in popularity ; and through the rest of the nine years during which they were associated, " A.B. and C.B." shone as equal stars in the free-thought firmament.

This result was not achieved without hard work. It meant writing up news and articles for press as fast as ever the material came in, and it meant travelling long distances on winter nights, in the icy, wooden-seated, third-class carriages—more like horse-vans—of those days, to remote country stations from which she was driven to the place of meeting in the butcher's cart ; it meant facing angry crowds, sometimes armed with chairs and stones. But Mrs. Besant was never afraid of opposition, or of hard work, and she had a superb constitution which never quailed before any amount of fatigue, and never, apparently, caught cold. The only occasions on which she became ill were those when some torment of the mind upset her body ; and she managed, generally, to get through as much work as any two or three ordinary men. A less pleasant fact was that she managed to create a certain amount of ill-feeling on the way to her position of prominence. Certainly she had risen very rapidly, and there were some eminent Free-thinkers who considered themselves slighted. Nor can it be said that Mrs. Besant always made things easy for them. Tact was never her strongest point ; she could argue with people or charm them, but she could not coax them, nor could she remember not to tread on their toes. If she thought they were foolish she said so and risked the consequences—or perhaps it would be more correct to say, never thought of the consequences at all. Therefore each phase of her career made her enemies as well as friends, though for the most part her enemies had ceased to be enemies before her life ended.

Whatever others might think, Charles Bradlaugh had no doubt about the qualities of his new helper. From the moment of his return from America he treated her as his equal partner, and the two of them laboured night and day in the cause of free-thought. They wrote, they spoke, they published ; they worked night and day, their only relaxation being when Bradlaugh went fishing and Mrs. Besant watched him from the bank. Nor was she merely a lieutenant ; he took her advice also on a number of matters, particularly in publishing a book on birth-control which landed them both in the law courts. Mrs. Besant in that suit defended herself, to the admiration of the judge and with such skill that the charge was finally withdrawn. The case, however, resulted in her losing her daughter, who was removed from her and sent back to Mr. Besant, on the ground that her mother was a wicked woman and unfit to have charge of a child. Mrs. Besant was very angry and indignant, and no doubt felt that she was bitterly unhappy. But she seems to have recovered quickly, and it may be doubted whether she was, in view of her many commitments and frequent absences on speaking tours, really the best person to make a home for a small girl. When they were free, on the death of their father some years later, to do as they pleased, both the boy and the girl immediately came back to their mother, which was at any rate a tribute to her.

For some years free-thought, birth-control, etc., filled all Mrs. Besant's time and energy. But it could not fill and satisfy her mind for ever. We may even be surprised that it filled it for so long, for, to speak truth, much of the early free-thinking and atheist propaganda of the time makes exceedingly dreary reading nowadays. There is little that is light or humorous about it, and we cannot think why people should have fastened on it with such avidity. We have to use our imaginations to see that, as I said before, it appealed as a message of hope and of struggle against tyranny, to understand why people crowded to listen to Charles Bradlaugh and to Annie Besant. When, in 1880, Bradlaugh was dragged by force from the Parliament to which he had been duly elected, there was a great tense crowd of working men waiting angrily in the street below who, at a word from Mrs. Besant, would have stormed the House of Commons to prevent the triumph of what they all felt to be oppression.

But already by 1880 a rival to the free-thought movement was making its appearance. The Socialists were beginning to say that the great oppressor of the poor was their poverty, and that the only way in which really to end oppression was to end poverty. Karl Marx, exiled from France and Germany and spending long years in the British Museum working out the doctrines of Marxian Socialism, had already gathered round him before his death, in 1883, a little group of propagandists of whom William Morris, poet, artist, and designer, was the best-known ; and another small discussion circle of young middle-class people, including Mr. and Mrs. Sidney Webb and Bernard Shaw, were getting ripe to form the Fabian Society which had so much influence on politics after the end of the century. It was some time before Mrs. Besant was converted to Socialism. As often happens, reformers who cared passionately for one kind of reform were very hostile and resentful to those who supported another. If you have given your life to a cause, believing that it is the one thing that will save the people, it is disconcerting and irritating to be told that your cause is no use at all, and that only something very different will help the people. Bradlaugh detested the Socialists, and said so on many platforms and in many articles, and Marx called Bradlaugh " the huge self-idolator." And as these two movements were actually competing for members among the same people, there was a great bitterness between them, and Mrs. Besant, naturally, sided with the Free-thinkers. But free-thought was on the decline ; in England, at any rate, a good deal of the battle had been won, and Socialism, in the years from 1880 onwards, was growing fast.

For some time Mrs. Besant held out, but circumstances and her own desire to help the poor were too much for her. A comparatively minor incident paved the way. In 1884 she was a member of the London School Board, which managed the elementary schools of London. *Justice*, the Socialist weekly, had been campaigning for free meals to be provided for the poor children out of the rates, urging the cruelty and foolishness of paying for teachers and books for children who had had no breakfasts. The obvious sense of this has long been recognized by many who are not Socialists at all, and milk and dinners may now be provided out of the rates for poor children ; but at that time it was supposed to be a dangerous Socialist suggestion, and when Mrs. Besant proposed it on the London School Board she was attacked by indignant Free-thinkers.

Afterwards, in the spring of 1885, she heard that Bernard Shaw, whom she had often attacked both in the *Reformer* and in her own paper, *Our Corner*, was to address a meeting on Socialism, and at once she decided to go to it. The result Mr. Shaw shall tell in his own words :

" I was warned on all hands that she had come down to destroy me and that my cause was lost. I resigned myself to my fate, and pleaded my case as best I could. When the discussion began, every one waited for Annie Besant to lead the opposition. She did not rise ; and at last the opposition was undertaken by another member. When he had finished, Annie Besant, to the amazement of the meeting, got up and utterly demolished him. There was nothing for me to do but to gasp and triumph under her shield. At the end, she asked me to nominate her for election to the Fabian Society, and invited me to dine with her "—this being the beginning of a close friendship which lasted for many years ; in fact the chief

claim to fame of her magazine *Our Corner* is that it published the novels of Bernard Shaw when no other publisher would look at them.

Mrs. Besant was a great acquisition to the Socialist
cause. However eminent the members of the original
Fabian Society may have since become, hardly any one
had heard of them then. Bernard Shaw was an obscure
journalist, Sidney Webb a clerk in the civil service, his
wife-to-be an intelligent lady who had done a little social
work in rent-collecting and elsewhere. Annie Besant was
the best-known propagandist in England, the best woman
orator, and with her curly hair, her loose blouse and skirts
that did not trail, one of the most picturesque. She flung
herself into the Fabian cause, joined their " Model
Parliament " and took the office of Home Secretary and
made the dry facts and reports which the Fabians got
out into eager and flaming speeches in all parts of the
country. As always, the sight of what she deemed to be
injustice or cruelty roused her full forces at once. In
1887, a black, bleak winter of depression, the unemployed
men, who then had nothing to live on but charity, de-
monstrated in London. They marched through the
West End, and broke the windows of a London club.
Respectable London was frightened and horrified ; it
thought that revolution was breaking out ; and another
procession was charged by mounted police and one of the
unemployed men killed. Mrs. Besant rushed to the
rescue, organized a Socialist Defence League, collected

contributions, and formed a panel of people pledged to
find bail and pay the fines of those accused of disturb-
ance.

Her greatest effort of those days, however, was not
directly connected with Socialism at all. It was the case
of the London match-girls. In 1888 Mrs. Besant had
founded a new paper, the *Link*, which was intended to act
as a general crusader on behalf of all helpless and down-
trodden people who were unjustly used. It invited all
who had grievances or who knew of abuses to write to it
giving the facts, when it would publish them, and pillory
those responsible in its pages.

After the *Link* had been running for some time an ex-
army officer, H. H. Champion, who was a Socialist, suggested to Mrs. Besant that she should take up the case
of the girls employed by Bryant & May. This celebrated
firm was making very fine profits, illustrated by the fact
that their £5 shares were being sold for £18 on the
Stock Exchange ; but they then paid shockingly low wages
to the girls whom they employed, most of them being
lucky if they found 8s. or 9s. in their weekly pay envelopes.
Mrs. Besant promptly published these facts, and the firm,
after threatening a libel action, dismissed the employees
who had talked to her. But even the brief contact with
Mrs. Besant had roused a new spirit in those wretchedly-
paid creatures. When they heard that their fellows had
been sacked, they left their work in a body, and marched
across the City to Mrs. Besant's office in Fleet Street.

She did not fail them. The next number of the *Link* was rushed out, full of headlines and appeals to shareholders and to the public. Bradlaugh and other M.P.'s asked questions in Parliament, Annie Besant and her Fabian friends organized meetings, made speeches and collected money for the girls on strike. In less than three weeks the firm had given way to the storm of public opinion which she aroused ; they reinstated the dismissed girls, and " as a result of that fight," said a Labour official many years afterwards, " that factory is now one of the model factories ; every person employed there is a Trade Unionist, and as far as it is possible under present conditions to solve the unemployment problem, they have solved it for their own industry. That all sprang from the work Annie Besant started down there."

Nor was the case of the match-girls important for itself alone. It broke, for the first time, the crust of complacency under which better-off London lived, concerning itself not at all with the fate of its poorer brothers. Mrs. Besant's articles and speeches made it no longer possible for well-to-do people to pretend that they did not know there was anything wrong ; and her efforts on behalf of the match-girls were followed by efforts for tin-box makers, mutilated by unfenced machinery, for shop assistants, " living in " above the shops in which they worked and deprived of most of their wages by fines that were illegally imposed, and finally, by a campaign for a " Fair Wages Clause " in the contracts given out by the.

221

London School Board. This campaign was successful, and it is now the generally accepted practice of Government Departments and all respectable town and county councils to give no work to firms which do not pay the standard rate of wages to their workers. Now it is the practice ; at the time, however, the suggestion scandalized people who thought it was the plain duty of public bodies to buy the cheapest uniforms or bricks or school Bibles, irrespective of the wages of the workers who made them or the conditions under which they worked.

Annie Besant seemed now, in 1889, to be full set to become the most important radical leader in England, when all of a sudden her career was cut abruptly in half. Before then, she had parted company with Bradlaugh. It was inevitable, because of the bitter antagonism between the Free-thinkers and the Socialists ; it was impossible to work with both. Mrs. Besant felt the parting, after ten years of the closest and sometimes the most exciting co-operation. But her natural buoyancy, and the fact that she was leaving to devote herself to a new cause which both inspired her and used up all her energies, made it less hard for her than it was for Bradlaugh whom she had left. It is all the more pleasant, therefore, to see that Bradlaugh, who in many ways was a hard and opinionated man, did not show any public bitterness, supported her new activities whenever he possibly could, and when, in 1887, she finally resigned her post on the *National Reformer*, paid her a generous tribute in an editorial. Not until 1889 did he realize that the separation was final—rendered so by Mrs. Besant's taking a step which must have shocked the Free-thinker to his marrow. For in 1889 Mrs. Besant became a theosophist and joined the Theosophical Society.

I shall say little about this part of Mrs. Besant's life, partly because space is short, but mainly because the details of it are not of interest to any one but theosophists. To put the facts briefly, by 1889 Mrs. Besant was clearly feeling a very deep need of some external religious guidance. As my readers will remember, her mother had said of her, " Dear Annie has always been too religious " ; and now for fifteen years she had had no religion at all, for the Free-thinkers denied it and the Socialists gave her none. And, faced with the harshness and contradictions of the world, her own vigorous spirit began to falter, and to ask for guidance from elsewhere.

Modern theosophy was founded by a remarkable old woman, H. P. Blavatsky, in 1875. Its chief teaching, which it obtained in the main from Hindu religious beliefs, was the doctrine of reincarnation, that is to say, the belief that each soul has lived in the world a great many times, inhabiting different bodies, and that its fate in one incarnation depends upon its behaviour in previous ones. One's misfortunes to-day may therefore not be due to any bad behaviour of oneself to-day, or even to any injustice in the present world, but simply to one's own bad behaviour in a previous incarnation, say, at the time of the Crusades, for which one is now being punished. Knowledge of this, knowledge of the world, its past and future, can, according to this idea, be obtained by putting oneself under the guidance of those who know more, people called *gurus*, who themselves obtain their own knowledge from even more initiated persons called *mahatmas*. This is explained, and the method of seeking information set out, in writings which are very difficult for any one who is not a theosophist to follow, and which contain teachings which seem to ordinary people to be magic or mumbo-jumbo, however you like to put it. Mrs. Besant, however, in 1889 found it exactly what she wanted. She read Madame Blavatsky's book, found herself greatly interested, and when she met Madame Blavatsky, who had a remarkable power over people and a shrewder judgment of them than Mrs. Besant ever possessed, she at once fell under the spell and became an ardent disciple. Characteristically enough, she charged into her new sphere of activity like a bull at a gate. She resigned from the Secular Society, the Fabian Society, and the London School Board, and announced her intention of devoting her life to theosophy and to occult study. She was a brilliant capture for the theosophists, and swung into the front of the movement as easily as she had done in the case of the Free-thinkers years before. She was almost immediately recognized as a leader, and by 1907, after various stormy passages—for she did not lose her vigour and combativeness when she went out of ordinary politics—she was President of the Theosophical Society and in possession of its innermost secrets.

There, most people felt, her public career had stopped. If you had asked anybody, in the middle of the first decade of the twentieth century, what was going to become of Mrs. Besant, the reply would probably have been that she had been a remarkable woman in her day ; but that she had been foolish enough, when in her prime, to throw herself away on a religious sect in which people were not generally interested, and that no more would be heard of her. Your sage informant would have been wrong. Not only was Mrs. Besant about to stage a come-back which startled the world : the new development, as a matter of fact, came directly out of her theosophical interests.

The reason is simple. As I have already said, much of the teachings of Madame Blavatsky and the Theosophical Society was derived from Indian mystics. Mrs. Besant, who, many years previously, in the days when she was a violent reformer, had been deeply interested in the problem of India, decided to go to India and see it for herself. Her first visit was made in 1893, and thereafter, for a long time, she spent about six months of every year in India. Her original reason for going there was purely religious ; but she was not the woman to sit down and stare quietly at anything without taking some sort of active part in it, and pretty soon we find her founding a college for Indian boys, the Central Hindu College, in the old sacred city of Benares.

This effort by Mrs. Besant to educate Indians was quite unlike anything that any European had ever done before. Ever since we had conquered India, we had made some small efforts to educate a few—a very few— of the Indian children, Lord Macaulay, the historian, being particularly interested in this question. But all the education had been British and given from a purely Western standpoint. Indian civilization is very old, much older than ours, and the Hindu religion is much older than Christianity. One might have thought, then, that the people who planned to educate Indians would have at least taken some notice of the Indians' own ancient culture ; but they took none. They simply treated these ancient traditions as though they were some low form of savagery, like cannibalism, for example, which ought to be stamped out, if possible, and if not, ignored. It is true that Hindu tradition contained some things which would certainly shock us—the habit of marrying children when they were very young, for example, and the way in which women were despised and thought of no account—but there are things in European civilization which would equally shock a Hindu, and the Indians felt it a deep insult that all they had been brought up to believe should be brushed aside as though it was just savage superstition.

Mrs. Besant felt quite differently towards them. Because so much of what she now believed came from Hindu sources, she was prepared to treat their traditions with the greatest possible respect—at one time she felt that, except for her white skin, she was herself practically a Hindu ; and so she insisted that at the Central College, and at other institutions which she founded subsequently, study of Hindu religion should be as important as study of the Christian religion was in English schools. Starting from this assumption, she was then able to suggest that parts of the Hindu tradition such as those mentioned in the previous paragraph were unpleasant and disastrous, and she found, as indeed might have been expected, that a number of the more intelligent Hindus agreed with her, and were quite prepared to take part in reforming these abuses, provided their backs were not put up by being called barbarians at the start. The Central College grew and flourished, and other colleges and schools with the same ideals were founded in India and Ceylon.

But Mrs. Besant did not stop there. Her work in school and college had convinced her that what was really needed was some sort of self-government for the Indians, so that their education would not end in futility, but would be directed to making them the sort of men and women who could really do things for themselves, instead of obediently performing such tasks as their British masters should order ; and accordingly, in the years just before the war, when she was already over sixty, she began an agitation for Home Rule for India, and got the Indian National Congress, the only body in

India in which native Indians had the opportunity of free discussion, to join with her. By 1913 she had already a scheme prepared, and though nowadays, when an enormous Government of India Act has been passed into law (in 1935) after discussion with many representative Indians, this may sound a small thing, before the war it was almost revolutionary. But Mrs. Besant was never deterred by appearing revolutionary; in the midst of her theosophical work she poured out books and pamphlets explaining to English people the claims of the Indians they had conquered to have a say in the way they should be governed.

The European War helped this work. Great Britain was, of course, very anxious that India should remain loyal, and should make, also, some contribution to the cost of the Allied forces. Mrs. Besant, who was wholeheartedly in favour of the Allied cause, felt that, if Great Britain wanted Indian support, she must do something to make the Indians feel that they were valuable allies, and not simply subjects who existed to be ruled and to be grateful for it. Pretty soon she reached the conclusion that not only was it the right and generous thing to offer some form of Home Rule to the Indian people, but that, if something of the sort were not done, there would be something like a new Indian Mutiny, which would be absolutely disastrous to Great Britain in the midst of a world war. For it would have been very difficult to spare troops from the Western Front to put down an

Indian revolt ; while, on the other hand, the enemy States would not have been slow to come to the assistance of rebels in India. Accordingly, in 1915 and 1916 she went about all over India, stirring up agitation and forming Home Leagues in different towns and districts, until the Government, which knew very much less than she did about the feelings of Indians, took fright, and became convinced that she was a dangerous woman who was trying to make India revolt from the Empire. Without warning, they shut up Mrs. Besant and two of her chief associates, not in prison, but in a place where they could write no articles, make no speeches, and see no friends. (This was called " interning " during the war ; it was done to persons whom the Government thought dangerous, as, for example, people of German birth who had become naturalized citizens of Great Britain, but whom, for various reasons, the Government did not wish to bring to trial in the courts.)

The Government " interned " Mrs. Besant ; but they did not realize, until they had done it, what they had done. Before she disappeared into captivity, she wrote a farewell address, which ended as follows :

" I go into enforced silence and imprisonment because I love India and have striven to arouse her before it was too late. It is better to suffer than to consent to wrong. It is better to lose liberty than to lose honour. I am old, but I believe that I shall see Home Rule before I die.

If I have helped ever so little to the realization of that glorious hope I am satisfied.

"Varde Mataram. God save India."

At once there broke out a terrific agitation. India was aflame ; questions were asked in Parliament ; even in that most august body, the House of Lords, there was an excited debate about Mrs. Besant. One very high official was said to have remarked in disgust to another, " Whoever would have thought that there would have been such a fuss over an old woman ? " But the fuss was effective. In 1917 the British Secretary of State for India, Mr. Edwin Montagu, was due to visit India and to meet persons of all sorts, in order to ensure that the three hundred millions of Indians remained loyal to the Empire. Before he went, he announced in a public speech that Great Britain's object was to give self-government to the Indian people ; and before he went, it had been arranged that, in order that his meetings should be tranquil and that he should have the confidence of those whom he met, Mrs. Besant should be set free without conditions. She was set free, and she returned to Madras in a triumphal procession ; it was an hour before the car which bore her was able to get through the cheering crowds. At the end of the year she was elected President of the Indian National Congress, an honour which had never been accorded before to any woman, and probably never will again. In eastern countries, women are kept

ANNIE BESANT

in harems or zenanas, and never supposed to show their
faces in public affairs. The election of Mrs. Besant was
as extraordinary as though a private soldier had been
chosen to be Prime Minister of this country.

Here we may take leave of Mrs. Besant, at the final
peak of her career. Not that her life had come to an end ;
in 1924, the jubilee year of her entrance into politics, a
great meeting of people in every walk of life assembled
in the Queen's Hall, London, to do her honour ; and in
1927, when she was already eighty, she was touring
America, and speaking at propagandist meetings literally
all over the world. But her work in India still remains
the last great event of her life ; it secured for her the warm
praise of a late Viceroy of India, Lord Willingdon, who
hoped that " she may be long spared to help in guiding
India " ; and though she did not, as she had hoped, live
to see Home Rule for India (for the Government of India
Act, which grants it in part, was passed in 1935, and
Mrs. Besant died in 1933), she came much nearer to the
realization of her hopes and desires than is granted to
most of us.

Perhaps the best comment on her whole life was given
by herself at her jubilee meeting. Moved almost to tears
by the tributes which were paid, she recalled how " when
Herbert Burrows " [a very old comrade and friend]
" and myself were walking in London streets, going back
from a meeting of omnibus-men who had no time to join
and work and plan for shorter working hours, and we

231

could only find them about midnight ; and as we tramped through the snow and the mud I turned to him and said, ' Herbert, I wonder why on earth we go on doing this,' and his answer was, ' We can't help it ! ' " That, I am sure, is the key to Annie Besant's life ; and few of us could hope to compose a better epitaph.

CLARE SHERIDAN

VIII

CLARE SHERIDAN

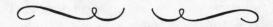

IT is well known to doctors and to health experts generally that there exist persons who act as "carriers" of the germs of certain diseases, who, without being ill themselves, possess continually the power to infect others. It is also known that there are some hereditary diseases which are not transmitted directly from parent to child, but sometimes skip a generation or seem to zigzag sideways like a knight's move in chess. Of such a kind is hæmophilia, that extraordinary affliction which is only found in men, and only inherited through women, who do not themselves suffer from it, but may hand it on to their sons. It ought, however, to be more realized than it is that of more pleasant things in life than disease there are "carriers"—people who, without themselves attaining to any especial distinction such as would get them mentioned in history books or in the *Dictionary of National Biography*, yet seem somehow to possess a tremendous flame of vitality which starts their descendants off in life with an endowment ahead of that of ordinary mortals, and capable of being turned to the most diverse purposes. It is not simply a question of inherited ability, as when great mathematicians or great musicians have mathematical or musical children, as they so often do, or when the sons and daughters of a painter show an aptitude for drawing ; it seems more as though the people that I mean are able to pass on to their descendants a store of personality and energy which has no special mark, but which can be used indifferently for art, music, literature, acting, politics, etc., as the children's tastes suggest when they grow up.

Of such a kind, it seems to me, were three American sisters who were educated in Paris towards the end of the last century, and who were known respectively as " the beautiful," " the witty," and " the good." They all married and brought up families : their name was Jerome, and they became respectively Lady Randolph Churchill, mother of Winston Churchill, Mrs. Leslie, mother of Shane Leslie, and Mrs. Moreton Frewen, mother of Clare Sheridan. None of these three ladies was herself particularly distinguished, except socially ; but to their offspring they seemed to have transmitted what the newspapers call " a whole galaxy of talent "—in several cases more than one talent to the same person. For instance, Winston Churchill is, of course, a brilliant politician. He is also, as many people know, a brilliant author of biography and reminiscences, and has, as not so many know, a gift for painting which he might have

developed quite remarkably. And his daughter has taken
up the stage as a career. Winston Churchill is the most
outstanding example of the children of the Jerome
sisters ; but there are others. And (not to make a long
and wearisome catalogue) Clare Sheridan, the subject
of this chapter, is a distinguished sculptor, has been a
distinguished journalist, makes much of her living by
literature, has travelled widely among all sorts of conditions, and is at the same time a *person* of quite outstanding individuality.

One more observation, before we turn to Clare
Sheridan's own life, ought to be made about the Jerome
offspring generally. Their gifts and their achievements
all seem to carry with them a suggestion of " amateurish-
ness " in the good and not the bad sense of the term.
(After all, the word amateur means lover ; and it is surely
rather unkind to assume that a man who loves painting
or sculpture is a man who does it rather incompetently !)
What I mean, however, is that they all seem to have taken
to their particular art because at the moment it happened
to suit them, because their great store of vitality could
most easily pour into that channel, and that it might, with
almost equal ease, have poured into another at another
time, when circumstances were different. They have done
brilliantly, because their natural gifts were brilliant—
and not, be it observed, without hard work. They have
not tried to cheat, or to perform without having learnt ;
but they have not been hag-ridden and driven, as the

237

lifelong artists are, by their work, forced to make experiments and to attempt tasks beyond their powers or their knowledge, to paint or write or carve things which they knew all the time would turn out badly and probably have to be scrapped, because only so, through experience and painful failure, could they learn enough to get on to the next stage in expressing the things they were trying to express. Clare Sheridan is an excellent sculptor of portrait busts : the likenesses and the general conception are very good, and they produce a sense of effortless mastery of the medium and the sitters which is very satisfying. There is, however, no trace, in her studio, of the extraordinary bits and pieces which other sculptors' studios contain, and which indicate the sculptor's effort to work in a new material, to try out a new arrangement of planes and surfaces, or to wrestle with the human body in new attitudes and at new angles. What is not portrait sculpture, there, is very nearly akin to it ; and her studio is the studio of a sculptor who models portrait heads, and devotes the rest of her life to other forms of living. For which there is a great deal to be said.

It seems to me that again and again in this book I have had to point out the extraordinary stupidity of the education of girls of the middle and upper classes during the past hundred years ; and I am rather afraid that my readers will heave a bored sigh at hearing that I propose to do it again. But I am not sure that Clare Frewen's education was not the silliest of all those of which I have read, mainly, I think, because being much younger than most of my other characters, she came at the tail-end of the period, when the idea that well-off women were meant for nothing more than to marry and live in idleness was just about to die, and when, consequently, the training or lack of training through which they were put was ceasing to have any particular meaning or to be really believed in by those who inflicted it. Lady Henry Somerset had a preposterous education, but at least it was the education that her mother intended her to have, and we have seen how ardently and closely her mother supervised it. But Clare Frewen's education seems hardly to have been supervised at all ; she had to be kept out of mischief by a nurse and then by a governess ; she had to learn something, preferably French and German, and then she had to acquire sufficient social arts and sufficient good looks to be sought in marriage by somebody, preferably an eldest son, who would be so much better off than his brothers. (In her book, *Nuda Veritas*, she has an amusing passage about the awkwardness of having anything to do with eldest sons, because your relatives were always watching anxiously to see whether you got on properly with them and ready to pat you embarrassingly on the back if you did.) The good looks were there all right ; but the social arts, as will be seen, were another matter.

One other thing I must mention about this late-Victorian and Edwardian type of upbringing, because it has struck me so strongly in re-reading it, is how *helpless* wealthy or near-wealthy people were—even more so than fifty years earlier—and what a lot of time and energy was wasted by the men in earning money wherewith to keep up large and inconvenient houses containing masses of " possessions "—glass and china and plate and books, which were in fact mostly kept locked or shut up in safes or cases where nobody could get at them—and in paying for staffs of servants to keep the houses and possessions swept and dusted, and to wait upon their helpless women-folk. The amount which was spent—and even, to this day, is still spent by some people—on the paraphernalia of living before you begin to enjoy life was colossal, and it was particularly hard on those who, while not possessing very much money or being careless with what they had, still had " a position to keep up," and so had to maintain large houses and staffs of underpaid servants, and buy a sufficient variety of expensive clothes to be sure of making their daughters attractive to suitable men. A good many of Clare Sheridan's early memories are coloured by the fear of bankruptcy, by the sight of bailiffs—" heavy, thickset men in overcoats, who sit in the best chairs, all hunched up and apathetic as if they had nothing to expect and nothing to say "—actually in her own home, by the necessity of cadging invitations from friends to lunch and dinner when funds were low, and by the terror that the sound of a pistol-shot might show that her father had taken one obvious way out of his difficulties. (For-

tunately he never did.) Even after her marriage to an
impecunious younger son, who was, nevertheless, earning
with great efforts an income which to many would have
appeared handsome, he and she were both burdened with
the necessity of keeping up a house with five servants and
the appropriate number of dishes for dinner, mainly
because Wilfred Sheridan's mother and sister had always
lived thus. After a long time, Clare Sheridan at length
released herself from this tyranny of mingled pomp and
helplessness ; but even for her, who was obviously a
natural rebel, quite vigorous shocks were needed to complete her emancipation.

Nor, with all that expenditure, was there as much
ease or pleasure as there is in many quite small homes
to-day. She was born in a house just off Park Lane,
which was then an extremely aristocratic neighbourhood ;
but the house was built so as to turn its back on the sun,
so that it was nearly always half-dark, and the nursery
in which Clare and her brothers Hugh and Peter were
brought up was lit by a leaky gas-jet, which stank. In
all her early years she only saw the country once, and had
to content herself for spring with the daisies in Hyde Park.

At the beginning she and her brothers were in charge
of a nurse who, as used at any rate to be the way with
nurses, was very much more interested in the little boys
than in the little girl, particularly as the little girl was a
vigorous child who had never caused any one any anxiety
on the score of her health. When Clare and Peter were

seven and six respectively, the nurse's reign came to an end, and they were handed over to a " Mademoiselle," who had practically sole responsibility for them for the next five years of their life.

A " Mademoiselle " of those days was a type whom one would hardly meet to-day. She was paid to relieve parents of all the care of their children, which they found a bore—nowadays parents, even if they thought their children a bore, would hardly dare to say so !—and to teach them something if she could. Particularly, for the children of the " upper classes," foreign languages. But, in accordance with a bad old tradition which had come down at least since the eighteenth century, she was paid very badly, and was never treated in any way as an equal by the parents, who would never have dreamed, for example, of inviting her to sit in the drawing-room or to meet their friends. This system gave the " Mademoiselles' " charges no natural respect for them, and was cruel to both. It was not the " Mademoiselles," however, who were to be blamed. The blame rested rather with the system, and with the parents who lazily accepted it. One blessing, at any rate, Clare Frewen derived from those five years—a profound alliance and friendship with her brother Peter, which has never since been broken or even bruised.

The children did not spend all those years immured in a narrow London house : they were, in fact, whisked about all over the place, from a lodging-house at East-

bourne to a castle on the Rhine, and back again to a
recently inherited Irish property at Innishannon near
Cork, where there was so much space and so many
opportunities to escape that even Mademoiselle's reign
lost some of its terrors. Indeed, about the time when she
disappeared from their lives, and when Peter Frewen
went off to join Shane Leslie and his other cousins at
Eton, the Frewen family must have been feeling wealthy,
for they possessed no less than three establishments—the
estate at Innishannon, a large London house in Chesham
Place, and a fourteenth-century house, half-ruined, called
Brede Place in Sussex, which was afterwards honoured
by visits from many literary lights, including that curious
and involved American novelist, Henry James.

Education—even a no-education—comes to an end
at last ; and after two more years under a succession of
governesses and two at a French convent school, where
she was homesick, bored with her lessons, and resentful
of the privileges that her parents had bought her of eating
meat on Fridays and having a bath twice a week (because
this rendered her conspicuous as a non-Catholic and a
heretic), Clare Frewen, at sixteen, came home, "finished."
Just before her education ended, during one of her
holidays, she had refused to be confirmed, saying that she
was going to become a Catholic. Upon which her mother,
when she had got over the first shock, commented, " It
is better to be a Catholic than to be nothing at all, but
it will make it very difficult for you to get married in

England." This sentence deserves to be pondered upon very slowly and deeply ; it sums up an age in English life.

Clare Frewen " came out " in 1903. The coming-out may have been less of a failure than she paints it in her autobiography, for one has to discount the modesty of persons writing their own lives ; but certainly she did not act in a manner calculated to enable her to make a good marriage and so to repay the amount which had been spent, not on her education, but on her clothes and keep. For one thing, she was still growing, and nobody who cannot remember Edwardian party clothes, with their elaborate cut, their belts and hooks and fichus and sashes, can realize how awkward that was. For another, she could not help giving herself away when she was bored ; but, worst of all, she showed signs of fancying herself in love with a young man called Wilfred Sheridan, a descendant of Richard Brinsley Sheridan, the great dramatist, who had only £500 a year and no particular prospects. What worse could she have done ?

She was sent away from London, half-disgraced as a failure, and for the next few years there is little that I find very noteworthy in her life. She drifted about from place to place, and from interest to interest. She had a season in Dublin, and she stayed with her mother in Malta, where she danced with the officers of the British Fleet, until the Fleet suddenly sailed away. She tried to paint, but met with no great success ; and she also tried to write. She earned ten pounds for an article ; but when she wrote a novel, George Moore, to whom she submitted it for criticism, told her that his first thoughts were, " What a dear little book she has written and what a charming girl she must be to have thought so well, so truly and so prettily." The comment was probably intended as praise ; but it made the " dear little girl " so indignant that she threw down her pen for a very long time. She also met, and became very much devoted to, Princess Margaret of Connaught, who is now the Queen of Sweden ; and this is of some importance, because it was the Queen's physician, Dr. Axel Munthe, who first gave her the idea that the elaborate paraphernalia of existence in which she had been brought up were not really necessary. He believed in living simply, in not possessing more than you could really use and in giving the rest away. He had considerable hypnotic power and could obviously gain an influence over people fairly easily; nevertheless, this type of advice was exactly what Clare Frewen needed. When she came to stay in a house belonging to him on top of a cliff near Capri, she was ready to do as he told her, give away all superfluous cash and live on meals consisting of only one dish—which is more easily done in Italy, where they know how to cook *risotto*, than in England, where they do not ; and the clearest sign of Dr. Munthe's effect on her was that almost immediately upon her return to England she married the " ineligible " Wilfred Sheridan. Even her wedding-day was not without its grim comedy, for the small girl who brought her wedding-dress in a band-box refused to leave it until it was paid for in cash, and her mother had hastily to go round to the bank and get the money.

Clare Sheridan's married life was short, and troubled in many ways. She was married in 1910—a wedding as slap-up and Society as could be managed—and she and her husband went to live in a Tudor house on Lord Midleton's estate in Surrey, which she soon found damp and dismal in an English winter, and lonely, when Wilfred was absent from morning to dusk earning the where-withal to keep up a "respectable" establishment. Not much chance of Dr. Munthe's simple life there ! After two years of it a daughter, Margaret, was born, and a year later another, called Elizabeth, who died early of meningitis, after a few months of life and illness. Hardly had the mother begun to recover from the shock of her second baby's death when the European War broke out, and before long Wilfred Sheridan had joined the army. He sailed for France in May 1915, and came back on leave in August, hoping to be home for the birth of his third child. But the latest male to bear the name of Richard Brinsley Sheridan shared the lot of many children born between 1914 and 1918. When he was two or three days old his father was killed, though his mother and grandmother did not know this until several days later, and wrote daily letters to the front describing the son's attractions—which letters afterwards returned in a bundle from France with the words " killed in action " written across them in red pencil. With a baby of a week or two old and a small girl of five, Clare Sheridan was left a war-widow, with a captain's pension, a father who, having played his part in bringing her up for the marriage market, could do very little else to help her, and a father-in-law who, owning an eleven-thousand acre estate in Ireland which had fallen on evil days, could do nothing at all.

Of course she was not likely to starve, nor would she have been allowed to, however straitened the means of her relatives ; but on the pension of a captain's widow, with war prices rising every day, she looked like being pretty badly off. To understand the way in which she avoided this fate we must go back a little, to the time after the death of the baby Elizabeth.

Immediately after the tragedy, Wilfred had taken her to Italy to recover from it ; and on her return the chief project which filled her mind was that of finding a memorial to her baby girl. She did not want anything like the heavy marble slabs and crosses and statues which fill so much of our cemeteries. "I felt that Elizabeth should have something different." So she went to the pottery works founded by G. F. Watts, the painter, at Compton, a few miles from her home, intending to choose from among the beautiful designs put out by Watts and his successors something which would fall in with her ideas. But while she was there Mr. Nicol, the manager of the works, suggested that she should take home a few pounds of clay and try to model a tablet or panel for herself, lent her a modelling tool, and gave her various hints on how to set about it. She leapt at the idea of trying to *make* something, however amateurishly, for Elizabeth instead of buying it ; and when she got her clay home and began to play with it, she realized that Mr. Nicol had done much more for her than help her to make a memorial ; he had given her a medium. The feel of the clay under her hands, the discovery that " mere mud " could be turned into tangible shape, still more, that it would at her dictation take the shape of Elizabeth's features—these gave her the authentic thrill of creation. After Elizabeth's panel was finished she went on working as a student at the Guildford Technical School three mornings a week and all her spare time at home. " There were moments," she says, " when a flame seemed to leap up inside me. . . . I knew it was a real vocation, that although it had come late it had come to stay. I had found myself at last."

The gift that she had found undoubtedly saved her from breaking down in the spring of 1914 : it was to save her again more than two years later ; but at first she did not realize this. After she had recovered from the shock and the birth of her son Dick, she lived for a while with her children cramped into her parents' house, contemplated the solution which most people would have suggested for her difficulties—a second marriage—and

CLARE SHERIDAN.

even got so far as to become engaged to a young soldier with a great deal of money, most of which he was apparently prepared to spend in showering gifts upon her. " I had so often thought," she writes rather ruefully, " what fun it would be if one could go into a shop and just buy anything one wanted. It is worth while to have done this in order to know how quickly the fascination can wear off and how sick of spending one can become."

It was certainly not greed for presents, rather a feeling of maternal affection and gratitude to the young man for playing so charmingly with the children, that had led her to think she could bear to marry him ; but as the time went on she came soon to feel that it was impossible, and she decided to break it off and to try and lead an independent existence. The young man, though believing himself broken-hearted, was engaged within ten days to somebody else ; and Clare Sheridan, in a comparatively short time, had established herself in a studio near Regent's Park, leaving her children in her mother's house, and was endeavouring to make a name and a living by modelling.

Of course in some ways she was fortunately placed. She had some money, if not much ; she could, for instance, afford to employ a maid in her studio, though to live with only one maid would seem the most horrible squalor to the people among whom she had been brought up. She had her mother's house in which to park her children, so that she could love them without their interfering with her work, which even the least cynical must admit to be an advantage. More important, perhaps, she had influential friends whose names were well-known to the public, and who, as they began to recognize her ability, would offer to sit to her and would recommend her to other clients. And, finally (to anticipate a little), she had a really remarkably piece of good luck when an American colonel on leave, who regarded her as one of the victims of a war for democracy, with that simple generosity which some Americans do possess and which makes them seem like fairy godfathers come to life, presented her with a thousand pounds on condition that she gave up pot-boiling and devoted herself to sculpture.

This is not to say that life was not hard at first. For she did not begin by getting commissions ; she had to earn and study at the same time, and she had to earn, not by sculpture proper, but by doing decorative modelled work which she managed to place with shops, such as picture-frames garlanded with fruit, painted terra-cotta pots, book blocks and plaques with small models in relief, etc., etc.—mostly things which were of no interest to do and of no value to the development of an artist. They took much time, and brought in little money ; nor indeed was the " real " sculpture always remunerative. People who could well afford to pay tried to get commissions done free ; and sometimes there were other troubles, as in the case of the lady who, admiring the model of her child's head in clay, asked to have it done in marble, and then paid neither for the clay nor the marble—which expensive material the artist had to buy. (Many people do not realize how expensive it is to be a sculptor, as compared with being either an artist or a writer. Clay, indeed, is not dear ; but bronze and marble and other such materials cost a great deal. Moreover, sculpture is awkward and expensive to carry out—to take or send to exhibitions, for example ; it cannot be piled into the motor cars of friends, like pictures, or sent through the post like a book. Much of the sculpture which Clare Sheridan did on her visit to the U.S.A. she gave away to friends before she left, to save the expense of taking it to England.)

Nevertheless, on the whole her work and career progressed with extraordinary rapidity. That brilliant easy mastery of which I spoke at the beginning of this chapter made itself apparent almost at once. Artists of repute like John Tweed and Professor Lanteri were anxious to have her as a pupil in their studios ; she obtained such important commissions as that of a bust of Asquith for the Oxford Union ; and by 1920, when she had been barely four years at her new job, she had already been offered an exhibition in a Bond Street Gallery. Discussing with a friend what heads she would like to include in that exhibition, if possible, she mentioned the name of one Krassin, a trade delegate from the U.S.S.R., who had just arrived in London—and thereby prepared for herself a jolt in her life, and, in fact, a new career.

It was 1920. The Bolshevik Revolution was barely two and a half years old ; it was only a few months since the British troops who were trying to destroy the new Russian government had been withdrawn from Russia, and the world as a whole was still expecting its speedy collapse and regarding Russia as a country of starving lunatics ruled by devils. If a bust of Krassin had been modelled and had appeared with horns, and flames coming out of its mouth, the British public would hardly have been surprised. Clare Sheridan, who had been fascinated by Russia and Russian stories since babyhood, but knew no more about the Revolution than the majority of her fellow-countrymen, was none the less " insatiably interested." She wanted to model Krassin ; she got an introduction to the Russian Soviet offices in London, and waited there, not perhaps quite certain whether she was going to be eaten alive or sent by some mysterious means immediately to Siberia.

She was not eaten ; far from it. For, besides Krassin, she met Kamenev, the head of the Russian delegation, and he, after giving her some sittings and seeing her studio and her work, suggested that she could come to Russia. " How can I ? " said she ; and he replied, " I will take you to Russia, and I will get Lenin and Trotsky to sit for you."

One must get back to the feelings of those years to realize what this meant. To-day, we all, whatever we may think about the Union of Socialist Soviet Republics, know that it is a great and extraordinary experiment which has certainly come to stay ; but in 1920 Lenin, whose embalmed body now lies in the Kremlin for thousands of his ardent admirers to look upon every day, was a sort of bogyman to Western Europeans. Hardly any one knew anything about the new society which the Russians were trying to make, and nobody but a few crazy Socialists had a good word to say for them. Clare Sheridan, with only Kamenev's word to protect her, and a very great doubt whether she would ever, if she started, get beyond Sweden, was invited to fling herself into this unknown country, where food, clothes, and all the amenities of life were said to be non-existent. She did.

The full story of her Russian experiences must be read in her own autobiography—of how she travelled there with Kamenev and innumerable Communists ; how in Reval she had her first experience of the Russians' complete indifference to time, food, and thick Russian tobacco-smoke when they are having a discussion ; how Kamenev's wife received her with cold and bitter suspicion ; how she did portrait busts of all the chief leaders of the Revolution ; how she nearly went with Trotsky to the front—but her heart failed her at the last moment ; and what Russia was like in those days of cold and shortage, poor food, clothes, soap, paper, and quantities of things which we take for granted almost unobtainable—and of unbounded enthusiasm.

It " got " her, however, as any one can see who looks

at the work which she did there. With the exception of the figure of Gandhi, the Russian portraits are the best work which she has ever done. And this is not necessarily because they " came easily " ; Trotsky's head, she says, was one of the most difficult. It got her, first because she was fired by the enthusiasm which she saw among them. She has always been ready to recognize and welcome vitality wherever she has found it, the consciousness of purpose, and devotion to a cause in which you believe ; and she found it at its highest among the Russians of the Revolution, slaving night and day without rest or thought for themselves in their eagerness to get on with making their new world. She paid no more attention than they did to the hardships and discomforts of a country struggling to consolidate a revolution when exhausted by war and civil war and still the prey of invading armies from outside—though she noted that it was not only Communism, but Russian ways, such as the unconsciousness of time, etc., mentioned above, which were particularly rough upon Westerners.

She is, I think, a natural Communist, though she never had any idea of, or wish to know the theoretical side of Communism or Marxism; but her sympathies were engaged at once. Particularly, she discovered, far more thoroughly than she had discovered from Axel Munthe's teaching, how pampered and helpless she still was, how little able to take care of herself—and how her life had been hamstrung and half-wasted because of sham values, of pretending to care for expensive possessions and belongings which she did not really want in the least, simply because all her acquaintances thought them important. When she started for Russia, she still thought it an appalling hardship to be given a bed in an hotel in which the sheets had not been put on freshly for her arrival ; after a little while she had discovered that in order to sleep it is not really essential to have sheets, or even a bed at all ; and that knowledge stayed with her, and was even intensified, after she had left the place where she learnt it. She was not the only person to find the artificial amusements and continual spending of London curiously meaningless and silly after the hard living and exciting purpose of Russia.

For the moment, after she had come back, she was News. A woman of the best families returned from the jaws of the wolves, and actually—so it was rumoured—having fraternized with them ! Possibly the crates which she was bringing with her and which she said contained busts of the Soviet leaders were really full of Russian crown jewels and the plans for the world revolution. At least, the Customs authorities made a very close and careful search of them ; reporters in droves met her boat at Newcastle ; and one of her friends carried off her diary for publication in the *Times*. There was a considerable sensation : some of her friends and acquaintances refused to speak to her, others said that all her information about Russia was entirely untrue—they, who had never been within five hundred miles of Trotsky, knew exactly what he was like : vindictive by nature, hideous in appearance, and monstrous to women. New friends appeared, Socialists and Communists whom she had never met before ; but only one, Krassin, instead of asking about Moscow, asked her for her impressions of London on her return. " I told him the shops seemed to me particularly stupid. So full of non-essentials." Krassin nodded. " I remember," he said, " I felt much the same when I returned to the world after being exiled in Siberia. I missed the simplicity and the inspiration of my Siberian life, and civilization seemed quite senseless." (A new light upon the advantages and disadvantages of exile.)

All this was no doubt very good for publicity, but it was not much good for work. So, acting on the advice of friends who thought it would be best to cash in on the publicity while the going was good, she accepted an invitation to go on a lecture-tour in the United States on her Russian experiences, and departed, taking with her Dick, now five years old. It was not a success. Quite simply, she disliked lecturing ; she disliked the Americans and the American press, American interviewers, and the foolish questions which Americans asked. She could not get her own feelings about the Russian Revolution across to audiences which were only interested to know whether or not she had met the Czar ; and very soon she was glad to be able to get out of her lecturing contract, and to stay in the States as a sculptor, the publicity she had already secured being sufficient to get her a good number of commissions to be going on with.

It was two years before she left America, during which she made time, as well as keeping herself and Dick by her work, to go for a long trip in Mexico, a country which she found as satisfactory as she found the United States distressing, and, on her return, to spend a few unforgettable days camping with Charlie Chaplin on a farm where interviewers could not reach him. But, except for these interludes, it was too much of a struggle. It was enormously costly to live in America in 1920–22 ; and, besides, it was bad for Dick and for Margaret, whom she had sent for during the second winter. She was really immensely relieved when Herbert Swope, the foreign editor of the *New York World*, who had read and remembered to some purpose her article on Russia, suggested that she should go to Europe on a commission from his paper, to write about whatever she thought interesting.

For six months Clare Sheridan was a journalist, the kind of journalist whom the American Press encourages much more than we do, who can go anywhere and write about anything, secure that his newspaper will give him plenty of space to say what he thinks. There have been a good many American journalists of this kind in recent years, some of whom, like Vincent Sheean, John Gunther, and Negley Farson, have subsequently published books which have been exciting best sellers. Clare Sheridan

257

owed her appointment in the first place to her ability to write vividly, which she had already shown, and in the second place to the vitality and quick capacity for interest which had impressed her American friends. The bare recital of her six months as a special correspondent is enough to make most people's mouths water.

She went to Ireland when the Free Staters and the Republicans were engaged in a last desperate battle as to whether the treaty with Great Britain should be accepted or not, and interviewed Rory O'Connor, one of the Republican leaders, in the Four Courts in Dublin a few days before the Four Courts went up in flames and six months before O'Connor himself was shot as a public enemy. She went on to Asia Minor, where the new Turkey of Mustapha Kemal was rebelling against the ferocious peace terms imposed after the war, interviewed Kemal himself—now the Dictator of Turkey—in Smyrna, and got into Mudania while the terms of the treaty which made Turkey into a nation were actually being discussed. She interviewed Stambulisky, the peasant Prime Minister of Bulgaria, who tried to make Bulgaria into a democracy of peasants, and was murdered a year later ; and she also interviewed Mussolini, who, she tells us, filled her with a great desire to laugh, " looking at me with fierce solemnity and enormous bulgy eyes that showed the whites all round them." After the six months was up she went to Germany (where Hitler had just made an ineffective attempt at revolution and every one was saying he was " finished "), and to Spain, where she interviewed a dictator who has since passed into oblivion, Primo de Rivera. Not a bad record for less than a year's work.

However, it had to come to an end. Even post-war Europe could not provide a sufficiency of journalistic *coups* to keep one for ever, and she had two children for whom she wanted to provide and to provide a home. England was unpleasant and expensive, the United States even more so. She tried a house on the Bosphorus, she tried Angora in Turkey-in-Asia. Finally—as she thought at the time—she hit upon Algeria, and decided to settle, Dick and Margaret and all, at Biskra on the edge of the Sahara, a place which Robert Hichens—earlier a great friend of hers—made known to everybody in *The Garden of Allah*. There she lived for eight years, getting into touch with Arabs and Arab life—in a way which she could not possibly have done except for her earlier experiences—and accumulating material which has since been written up in her book *Arab Interlude*, from which I wish I had space to quote here. One must, however, leave something over for people to read for themselves ; and readers who want to know what an Arab wedding is like, how muscularly weak Arabs are when pitted against athletic English girls, or what are the troubles of any one who tried to drive a car through the desert, must get that book and read it.

It is quite possible that Clare Sheridan believed, at the time when she went to Biskra, that she was going to end her days there in peace. But that, of course, as any one else could have guessed, was nonsense. She had had a wild and upsetting year, following upon a good deal of strain, from which she needed time to recover. But by 1931 she had heard of Mahatma Gandhi and discovered that he was going to attend the Indian Round Table Conference in England, and at once she set off to find him. The bust of Gandhi is one of the best things that she has ever done, part of the reason being, I think, that she has a natural leaning towards Indian mysticism; she counts herself a believer in reincarnation, and would probably, had she ever met Mrs. Besant, have become a theosophist. But be that as it may, after she had finished Gandhi she found that to vegetate in Africa was not really what she wanted. She made over the house at Biskra to Margaret, now about to marry, and herself returned to England—but it is characteristic that, stopping in Paris on the way, she was just in time to see the riots of February 1934, which came very near to making France a Fascist country. This was barely three years ago : it seems at least reasonable to ask, " What will happen next ? "

BEATRICE WEBB

BEATRICE WEBB

WHEN Beatrice Webb was informed that she was to be included in this book, her immediate reply was, " But how can you write about one of us without the Other One ? "

There is great point in this remark. For what one thinks of, in contemplating the careers of the two greatest social investigators of our time, is not of Beatrice Webb or of Sidney Webb, but of " the Webbs "—a single entity or combination which has done work which by no possibility could one of them have done alone. Of the eminent women here chronicled, some have been happily married, some unhappily, and two not married at all ; but of none can it be said that their marriage made them into something which they could not have become without its aid. And as marriage is still, and will probably continue to be, the lot of the majority of girls in Great Britain, it is really worth observing how immensely the right sort of marriage can increase the stature and develop the capabilities of the right sort of women. " Two second-rate minds," Mrs. Webb, with the characteristic Webb modesty, observes, "but curiously complementary." We shall see, having looked at Mrs. Webb's life both before and after her marriage, exactly what this means in practice ; in the meantime, it is not off the point to notice that, while one naturally tends to refer to Elizabeth Garrett and Mary Macarthur (both of whom were happily married) by their maiden names, nobody ever thinks of writing about " Beatrice Potter." She will be known to history, as she has been known to her contemporaries for forty-five years, as Mrs. Sidney Webb.

She was, however, thirty-four when she married Mr. Webb, and had therefore had a long time for development before she even met him. That development we must now trace ; and we shall begin by noticing with interest that Mrs. Webb, unlike most of the other characters in this book, had no natural tendency towards feminism and no particular quarrel with her upbringing. Indeed, in 1889, she actually signed a manifesto against the giving of votes to women, and though she afterwards decided that she was wrong, the fact that she signed it at all is interesting. The explanation, however, is not very difficult. She never suffered at all from domination by males : she had a father who, having nine daughters, was deeply convinced of the superiority of women to men and acted upon it, gave his daughters full freedom and discussed with them as though they were at least his equals. As she was not a man, moreover, public opinion did not force her to take up a money-making career, or make her feel a failure if she did not ; she could live on her father's earnings and do research (or anything else she chose) whether or not there was any money to be made at it ; and when she did take up research, she was given more attention and politeness than would have been accorded to a man. (Or so she thinks, though it may be suggested that the attention given was due at least as much to her own outstanding personality as to her not being a man.) The fact, however, is that she felt that her sex had been rather an advantage than a disadvantage to her, and that she was too honest not to admit it. Nor did she sympathize with those ardent feminists who declared that women were always and in every way the superiors of men ; indeed, that opinion is fairly obviously nonsense. But women who were told continually, from earliest infancy, that they were inferior to their brothers or husbands, tended to react violently against that view. Nobody ever told Beatrice Potter that she was inferior to any male : consequently she felt no need to assert herself and only found out fairly late in life that there were women, even the majority of women, who did.

Her childhood and youth were sheltered and secure, and if they were not altogether happy, that was mainly due to her own delicate health and introspective nature, rather than to any external force.

Her father was Richard Potter, son of a Radical, but himself of Conservative leanings, who was brought up to be a country gentleman, but after a financial crisis had to take to business, in which he was successful enough to keep up a big house and maintain a large family. With her mother she never really got on until just before her death. " She disliked women," Mrs. Webb writes sympathetically, in the first volume of her autobiography ; " and she was destined to have nine daughters and to lose her only son." Of her daughter Beatrice, Mrs. Potter wrote, " She is is the only one of my children who is below the average in intelligence," a misapprehension so startling that one does not wonder that they did not get on very well.

In this large family Beatrice, the eighth daughter, was a lonely child, lonely partly because she was delicate and frequently ill in one way or another—and normally healthy people do not realize how much ill-health sets one apart—partly because the brother who immediately followed her died at four years old, and partly because of a natural tendency to withdraw into herself, to brood in secret upon the mysteries of the world and upon her own faults and failures. For this last trait her biographers may well be grateful, since it caused her to keep intimate diaries which, when used for her autobiography, enable us to understand how this awkward, delicate, self-conscious girl developed into one of the most unself-regarding and effective workers of our time ; but it must be admitted that a child of ten who could write, " Vanity, all is vanity. I feel that I have transgressed deeply, that

I have trifled with the Lord. I feel that if I continue thus I shall become a frivolous, silly, unbelieving woman," was definitely in danger of becoming morbid. There was too much intelligence there, rather than too little.

After that entry, it is interesting—and rather re-assuring—to note that " the first scene I remember is finding myself naked and astonished outside the nursery door, with my clothes flung after me by the highly trained and prim woman who had been engaged as my brother's nurse " (what her sin on that occasion was she does not remember !) ; and that, being considered too young for the schoolroom, she then took refuge in the laundry, where she was made welcome, and where, " curled up amid rough-dried tablecloths and bedsheets, I dozed and day-dreamed ; or, sitting on the ironing-board swinging my legs, I chattered to an audience of admiring maids about my intention, when I was grown up, of becoming a nun." She at any rate did not suffer in the least from being " left to the charge of servants."

As to education in the more formal sense, she seems to have had little of it. She cannot remember learning to read ; at some stage or other she " drifted into the schoolroom," though before that she had begun to browse among the miscellaneous reading-matter, books, pam-phlets, and what not, that were stacked or scattered any-where about the large plain house in Gloucestershire where a good part of her childhood was spent—it is now a county hospital. Probably her health prevented her having many definite lessons ; and, apart from the real educational effect of many visitors and acquaintances of importance continually visiting the house and discussing matters with her father and mother—and with the girls as they grew up—she had little real mental discipline until she became the pupil of that odd product of Victorianism, the philosopher Herbert Spencer. Spencer had long been a friend and admirer of her father's, though Mr. Potter quite firmly, albeit good-humouredly, considered his philosophical theories nonsense—in which many would agree with him ; and Beatrice gradually became a kind of half-secretary to the old gentleman, developing an affection for him which lasted right to his death in 1903. At one time Spencer had appointed her his literary executor, but this he cancelled when she became a Socialist, for to Herbert Spencer Socialists were anathema.

He did, however, teach her a good deal. In particular, he taught her to respect and to hunt up *facts*—facts of all sorts bearing on the things about which she was going to write or discuss. Actually, Spencer himself had less regard for facts than she perhaps credited him with. He himself believed that he had arrived at his own peculiar theory about evolution by ruthlessly examining all the facts ; but the great Professor Huxley denied that utterly. " He elaborated," said Huxley, " his theory from his own inner consciousness. . . . He never reads, merely picks up facts to illustrate his theories " ; and it was

in the picking up of facts that Miss Beatrice Potter aided
him—a habit which was to be enormously useful to her
in her later work. And he, on the other hand, helped her
in the study of German and Greek philosophers, listened
and criticized her early scribblings about metaphysics,
and, in general, was the only one of her elders whom she
felt was really friendly and concerned about her per-
sonally. He was an odd old creature, full of knots and
cranks and perversities ; but one young woman had
cause to be really grateful to him. More than all,
perhaps, he set before his pupil " the example of continuous concentrated effort in carrying out, with an
heroic disregard of material prosperity and physical
comfort, a task which he believed would further human
progress." That lesson, at all events, was well and truly
learned.

It was some time, however, before the full fruits of
Spencer's education were garnered ; and she had no
other. Possibly, if she had had even a little more formal
education, and little of school and of the kind of work
which preparing for examinations means, she might have
been saved a certain amount of unnecessary trouble. For
instance, she was very slow in learning to read a document
quickly and get the sense out of it, which is an essential
qualification for a historian. Statistics, other than the
most elementary arithmetic, were beyond her ; for to
comprehend statistics you must at least know algebra,
and the only results of her first and last attempt to learn

algebra was that she saw a ghost in broad daylight! Further, she could not copy out extracts accurately, and if she did she could not read her own copy, for one of the most characteristic features of Mrs. Webb has always been her absolutely abominable handwriting, which makes a letter from her look like a cryptogram or an attempt to draw a maze—anything rather than a letter. On the other hand, she was not troubled by having to study English literature, which would certainly have driven her crazy, because she has always found poetry extremely boring, remarking that she could not understand what a poem meant until she had translated it into prose, and then it did not seem worth the trouble. I do not believe that Beatrice Webb (or Sidney either, for that matter) would turn a hair if they were told that all the art and literature in the world had disappeared : in fact, a friend of theirs recently remarked that, if they had been writing a book on England in the Age of Elizabeth, they would have lumped Shakespeare and all the poets, song-writers, and painters into one chapter along with the improvements in the sanitary conditions in towns, and called the whole thing " Amenities in the Elizabethan Age." It may be the same lack of sensitiveness to litera-ture which causes some of their books to be written in a remarkably heavy style, with ponderous winding sentences which leave the reader gasping and giddy long before he gets to the end. This is by no means true of all the books ; but nobody, I think, who was at all sensitive to the sound of words could write an important work on English eighteenth-century history, and send it out to the world under the unappetizing and almost unpronounceable title of *Statutory Authorities for Special Purposes.*

With or without education Beatrice Potter was designed to go into society and to marry—as, eventually, all the nine Potter sisters did ; and for a time she duly came to London for the " Season." She did not dislike it as violently as some of the characters in this book ; in fact, she appears at times to have looked forward to the parties and the general excitement of it. What she does note, looking back at it from the tranquillity of old age, was its enormous expensiveness, the amount of elaborate organization that was required ; and, rather more seriously, the competition in display, in clothes, food, wine, and flowers, the continuous attempt to show off more than somebody else, or to get more notice—or notice from " better people "—than any one else, which made " society " as much pain as pleasure for any one who had any share of personal vanity, and so could feel hurt if the notice was not forthcoming, or the clothes outshone by somebody else's clothes. She came to the conclusion in the end that " the pursuit of pleasure was to me a tiresome undertaking, entailing extensive plant, a large number of employees, and innumerable decisions on insignificant matters "—particularly after her mother's death in 1882, when she had to organize the " undertaking " herself. It was not that she was unpopular in any way ; she had striking looks, though she never learned, or never cared, to put her clothes on properly—H. G. Wells, in an unkind skit published thirty years later, spoke of her as looking like " an untidy eagle." She was intelligent enough for any distinguished man to talk to, though even then she was apt, if she found anybody foolish, to express herself rather more definitely than was agreeable to the other party. But, though quite respecting the brains and the ability of those whom she met in this way, she was bored—and that was that. The only advantage, I should say, that she retained from her society experiences was that, having once learned to " organize the under-taking," no other organizing, whether of households, parties, or societies, had any terrors for her. Others who, not so practical, have tripped up over the comparatively minor job of running their own homes, may envy her that bit of training.

By 1882, bored with pleasure-seeking, she had begun to contemplate doing some real work. For some time she had hoped (as others have hoped before her) to " write a great book " ; but what the book was to be about she (again like others) was not at all certain. But slowly, almost without her noticing, the subject of her life's work was beginning to press itself upon her. She began to be more and more interested in how the English world, the world which was made up of so many millions of her fellow-creatures, lived. Long before that date she had realized quite clearly that she belonged to a very small minority in that world, a minority distinguished not so much for its wealth—for the Potters, though they were undoubtedly well-off, were not encouraged to spend recklessly, except for very definite purposes—but because it possessed *power*. " My father spent his whole life *giving orders*. . . . My mother sat in her boudoir and *gave orders*. . . . I became aware that I belonged to a class of persons who habitually gave orders, but who seldom, if ever, executed the orders of other people." The contrast between the upper, and what the early Victorians used to call " the industrious classes," could not be better stated. Beatrice Potter, before she was twenty-five, had realized that this class which gave orders was a very small part of the nation, and had developed a curiosity to find out how the rest of it lived, and what it was like. From her father she had only learnt that it consisted mainly of a curious impersonal thing called " labour," of which she used to hear from him that " labour was docile " (or " restive," as the case might be), or that " the wages of labour are falling to their natural level." She had never realized that that " labour " consisted of millions of actual working men and women and their families.

She started by working in London with the Charity Organization Society. This was a body founded in 1869, by worthy persons who were convinced that the casual handing out of money to beggars by well-intentioned charitable people often did more harm than good, because

the most insistent beggars were often disreputable characters who preferred begging to doing any sort of work,
and who spent the money given them on anything which
took their fancy, and because the poor who really needed
help most were very unwilling to beg. This was partly
true ; but it was also true that at that time (as was
subsequently proved up to the hilt by Charles Booth in
the great investigations he made into the life of the
people of London) for every beggar who was undeservedly
helped there were hundreds who were in miserable poverty
through no conceivable fault of their own, but simply
because they were ill or out of work, or employed at
wages too low for them to live on. The charity of the
well-to-do, however well it was organized, could not
possibly help more than a fraction of these cases ; and
as the C.O.S. in the course of trying to organize it asked
a great many questions, many of them of the most
personal kind, of people whom it then decided not to
help at all, it quickly became unpopular among the poor
—particularly as some of its leading personalities could
never free themselves from the idea that if people were
poor it was in some way their own fault. Beatrice Potter
was partly saved from that narrow point of view by going
and staying at Bacup in Lancashire with some of the
working people from whom her own grandmother had
come. (In order not to appear to them as a " superior
person," she was introduced by her own old nurse, and
stayed among them, not under her own name, but as

" Miss Jones of Wales.") There she discovered that cotton spinners and weavers were real people : she lived among them, shared their meals, and discussed politics and the conditions of life with them. She found out what they thought about church and chapel, about their employers, and about their own lives ; she discovered their devotion to the " Co-op.," their own shop, where they provided themselves with the necessities of life without paying profits to a big store-owner, and to the Trade Union which protected their wages and conditions ; and this first-hand knowledge she never forgot.

For some years after her mother's death she was slowly feeling her way to the writing and investigation which she really wanted to do. The process was hindered to a certain extent by a paralytical stroke which befell her father in 1885. As she was the only daughter who was unmarried, this meant that from then until his death in 1892 much of her time was spent in looking after him, though her sisters to some extent shared the burden. In spite of this handicap, however, her self-training as a social investigator proceeded steadily. She spent a year acting as rent-collector for a block of gloomy flats, built as cheaply as possible to house poor families removed from the slums, and came to the conclusion in the end that they were of no use towards solving the problem of poverty.

In 1886 her help was sought by her cousin Charles Booth in making his great inquiry into the *Life and Labour of the People of London*, which was of such enormous importance for later investigators. This was work exactly after Beatrice Potter's heart. Before Booth started, people had made assertions from time to time about the conditions of the poor in London ; but nobody had really known much about it that was accurate or could be proved. Booth sent an army of investigators from street to street and from house to house, asking questions of everybody who might be presumed to know the answers, about what wages people received, what they could buy with them, what their houses were like and what they paid for them—with the result that he discovered, when his researches were completed, that nearly one-third of the entire population of the richest city in the world were living " below the poverty line," *i.e.* actually on less than would suffice to keep them in health enough to work. Since then we have had a number of such inquiries, and are more used to statistics of this kind ; but at the time Booth's results shocked even the complacency of Victorian London, and Beatrice Potter contributed a good deal to their compilation. She also investigated " sweating " (see the chapter on Mary Macarthur) in the East End, and worked for some time as a trouser-hand in an East End workshop, where she was not a successful workwoman, but overheard the wife of her employer saying to her husband, " She's no good at the sewing : if I keep her I'll put her to look after the outworkers—she's got the voice and the manner to deal with that lot "—a tribute which on the whole she did not appreciate. At the same time she found the opportunity to write a book on the Co-operative Movement, which has become a classic textbook and has been translated into many languages, and by 1889 was beginning to be recognized as an authority on " social problems."

But during this time two things were happening to her. She was coming more and more to feel that the problem of poverty, at least as she had seen it, could not be solved by charity from private persons or any similar means, but only by the State taking it in hand : in short, she was becoming a Socialist. And she was also trying to write a book which should tell the middle and upper classes about the organizations which the workmen had formed to protect themselves, about their history, what they were for, and what they really meant to the people who had made them. But this was an enormous task, involving not merely interviewing hundreds of Trade Union secretaries in distant and dismal towns, but also going through heaps of old and dirty documents, often hidden in damp cellars or other awkward places, files of ancient ill-printed newspapers, etc., etc. She was beginning to feel that she had set herself an impossible job, when she found her collaborator.

This is not a life of Sidney Webb, so I will content myself with pointing out that he is the complement of his wife in almost every possible way—even physically. She is tall and he is short : she is striking to look at, with a loud clear voice and a commanding personality ; he is very plain, with a large head and a tiny body, strong spectacles, a little wisp of a beard, and a rather weak throaty voice which is difficult to hear at any distance. Socially, he is of entirely different origin. Hers has already been described; he was the son of an accountant and a hairdresser in London, went to work as a clerk at sixteen, and through evening classes and an almost horrifying proficiency at examinations, forced his way into the First Division of the Civil Service and entered the Colonial Office. He possessed in full measure the gift of being able to read a document and gather almost at once precisely what it was about and what were its points of importance; and even his handwriting was the direct antithesis of hers, being large, round, and almost alarmingly clear. She met him first at the beginning of 1890, when he was recommended to her as an authority on the British working class in the nineteenth century. Thereafter they corresponded and their friendship grew; at Whitsun, "in the Glasgow streets, by glorious sunset, knocking up against drunken Scots, two Socialists came to a working compact." Beatrice warned him that "the chances are a hundred to one that nothing follows but friendship." He accepted the conditions, and steadily followed up every chance that came. In 1892, six months after Mr. Potter's death, *Fabian News*, the monthly journal of the Fabian Society, laconically announced that "Sidney Webb and Beatrice Potter have married one another." They set out together for Ireland, in order to combine a honeymoon with an investigation into Trade Unions in Dublin.

This will undoubtedly seem comic to a good many people, but it is absolutely and completely characteristic of the great firm of Webb which was born in 1892 and is now all but forty-five years old. They were two people who were very deeply in love—so much so that it is not much of an exaggeration to regard all those forty-five years as a prolonged honeymoon—and what they proposed to do with that honeymoon was to investigate the conditions and life of the working-classes of Great Britain, with the intention—and this is very important—with the intention of altering the policy of the country towards them. As I regard the Webbs as the people who will loom largest when some future historian comes to write the story of Socialism and the Labour Movement in this country, and also as one of the most outstanding examples of a perfect marriage partnership, I propose to say something about them in both those aspects. I shall begin with their work, not indeed in detail, because that would mean an enormous and boring catalogue, but in its general effect.

The work which the Webbs have done is of two kinds: practical organization, and the writing of books. Of the books I shall say little here, not because they are not of importance, but because they are for the most part solid and difficult reading—made more difficult by the curious Webb style to which I have referred before—and therefore not very likely to be read by young people. It will be enough to say that they include important and authoritative works on almost every subject which is of interest to students of politics, beginning with the big—and very readable—*History of Trade Unionism* which was their first joint book, including ten large tomes on the history of all the different parts of English local government, and ending with two volumes (for which they began the research when they were well over seventy) on *Soviet Communism*, which sum up all that was known at the time of their writing about the new Russian State. Nor are these books—which are only a selection of those they have written, without taking count of pamphlets and other minor works—just evolved out of their own heads, as one might write a novel ; they are the product of long and intense investigation, either by talking to all sorts of people, which is Beatrice's speciality, or by digging into and extracting facts from quantities of documents, in which Sidney excels.

These rows of books provide a library which any one who wants seriously to study English social questions will always—unless things change very much—have to master before he can be considered an expert. But if we leave all their books on one side, and consider only what they have done besides their writing, we shall find it sufficient for two or three ordinary lives.

Mrs. Webb, when she married, was a Socialist and a member of the Fabian Society : her husband was one

BEATRICE WEBB : MRS. SIDNEY WEBB.

of its founders. The Fabian Society, though small, was in its heyday a remarkable body. It consisted of a number of young intellectual persons, mostly writers and civil servants, who had come to the conclusion that Socialism, by which they meant the gradual taking over, by the State or by public bodies like County and Borough Councils and the like, of the principal industries of the country, was the only way in which the condition of the poorer classes of the people could be really or permanently improved. (There is no room here to explain more fully what they meant by this ; it is all now part of the programme of the Labour Party.) There was nothing very new in being a Socialist ; what was new about the Fabians was that they did not propose to make themselves a loud-voiced political party, waving red flags and trying to appeal to large mass meetings ; they intended to proceed quietly, by converting important people in the Government and the Civil Service, and by persuading all kinds of influential associations, bodies of teachers, or doctors, of all manner of professional men, County Councils, Trade Unions, and hosts of others, to support suggestions which led in the direction of Socialism.

This method of working—which the Webbs called " permeation "—could clearly only be applied by very highly trained and educated persons, who would know exactly what arguments would be best to use on whatever type of person they were trying to convince, and who would also know (what the most eloquent orators often do not know) when to stop arguing and leave the persons with whom you have been arguing to think the thing over quietly. They would also need, if they were to argue with distinguished Civil Servants and public men, to be very certain that their facts were right. For this job the early Fabians were very well equipped. They had Sidney Webb, who had an enormous appetite for facts, and (which is much more important in argument) could always remember them accurately ; they had Sydney Olivier, now Lord Olivier, who had had actual experience of government ; and they had the most brilliant of all Socialist propagandists, Bernard Shaw—and, for a while, Annie Besant. When they had added to themselves Beatrice Webb, with her knowledge of the actual lives of the poor and her power of being calmly rude to any-body who tried to oppose her, they were very nearly invincible. Indeed, between the 1880's and 1906, when a Liberal Government came into power, they had con-verted a surprising number of the "people who mattered"; and if the European War had not intervened we might have been to-day living in an England governed by Fabian Socialists. As it was, a considerable number of the reforms which they advocated have been put into effect by Governments which were not in the least Social-ist. This was very much in accord with the intentions of the Fabian Society. While the Fabian Society is affiliated to the Labour Party, and has always given it hearty support—in fact, when the Labour Party was reorganized

after the war Sidney Webb was mainly responsible for
drafting its new programme and its new constitution,
and was twice a Minister in a Labour Government—they
had always hoped to proceed towards Socialism as much
by persuading members of other parties to put bits of their
programme into effect as by the direct action of a working-
class party. There are limits, however, to what can be
done by this method, particularly in the post-war world,
where Fascism and armaments stalk abroad, and the
Webbs, at any rate, have been inclined, particularly since
they went to Russia, to lay less stress on the policy of
" permeation."

A history of all the organizations and causes which
they started during forty years would fill pages—one of
the largest still existing is the London School of Economics,
which now trains thousands of students yearly, and was
founded by the Webbs in two modest rooms by means
of a legacy left to the Fabian Society. Another is the
important weekly periodical, the *New Statesman*, which
goes on its way quietly eating up its competitors. But the
most important thing about their organizing is its *thorough-
ness*. When they had thought of a project and seen that
it was good they did not pass a resolution at a meeting
or write a letter, and leave it at that. They set to work
to bring it into being. They thought of all who would
be likely to be interested, all who might give money, if
money was needed, and all who would be opposed and
would have to be conciliated if possible. Then they gave

a lunch-party : they put their proposals forward. Sidney, having got up his brief in advance, was prepared with answers to every possible objection, and Beatrice bullied the great and the rich into doing what they were told.

When their project was launched they were ready to follow it up. They knew all the people and all the organizations, down to the smallest Trade Union branch, to which letters, circulars, and advertisements ought to be sent. They also knew the people who ought to write the circulars and the people who ought to be sent out speaking for whatever the project was. They, particularly Beatrice, had always a remarkable gift for getting hold of young enthusiastic men and women of ability and setting them to work. " Beatrice's young men "— some of them now very distinguished—used to be a by-word in the Labour Movement ; and it was not only brilliant young men whom they brought into their web, but typists, secretaries, note-takers, persons who would read newspapers for them and persons who would go out interviewing. No. 41 Grosvenor Road, the house on the Embankment where they lived for many years, came to be really the centre of a vast factory for making and developing Socialist projects and Socialist movements of all kinds.

Naturally, not everybody was as well satisfied with it as the Webbs. Their opponents complained that the pair of them behaved like a steam-roller, that they set everybody to work on the lines they chose, and sometimes for very scanty pay—for parsimony was always one of the

weaknesses of the Fabian Society ; that they had all
their arguments ready and never listened to any one
else's, so that, if they were really wrong on any point
(and no one can be always right) there was no chance of
convincing them of it. Finally, that they were deaf and
blind to all the finer values of existence, and that the
society they hoped to make would be more like a well-fed
ant-heap than a home for humanity. All these criticisms
may be found expressed in the amusing but bitter satire
on them which H. G. Wells wrote in a novel called *The
New Machiavelli*. The Webbs showed no sign of minding
this attack, any more than they have minded others—in
fact, one exasperated controversialist once said of Sidney
that he was like one of the children's toys whose bases
are loaded with lead—however often you knocked him
down he always came up again exactly the same.

This enormous imperturbability has, in fact, been one
of the Webbs' greatest assets. It is impossible to find in
them any trace of bitterness, even towards those with
whom they most profoundly disagree or who have most
bitterly attacked them. This calmness of temper, which
has obviously saved them both much pain and much
waste of time, comes, I suggest, directly out of the extraordinary happiness of their marriage.

From Beatrice's autobiography—Sidney keeps no
diaries and does not chronicle his feelings, so one has to
guess whether or not he is happy—it is quite clear that
marriage made her, and that from being a person of

worried, introspective mind who might have ended anywhere, she became, almost at a stroke, one of the happiest
people in the world. The main reasons were, in the first
place, as I have said before, that they were so exactly
complementary, one bringing what the other one lacked ;
in the second, that their marriage was a partnership
between two reasonable people who intended to get on
and do their jobs, and who would have regarded the sort
of bickering and quarrelling which too often takes place
between married couples who are very much in love with
one another as simply a foolish waste of time and energy ;
and in the third, that they were absolutely agreed both
on the work they wanted to do and the kind of life they
wanted to lead.

They had about £1,000 a year, unearned, between
them. They decided that that was enough, expended on
plain living without frills, to enable them to do what they
wanted without troubling about money, and to take
" such recreation as would keep them in reasonable
health "—the phrase is Sidney's. Fortunately, they liked
the same kind of recreation ; they liked bicycling, travelling for the purpose of making political studies, entertaining young people—and old people—who would be useful,
and talking politics. Neither of them had any inconvenient tastes which would have interfered with the comfort of the other ; and fortunately, again, Sidney either
liked, or at all events acquiesced in, whatever Beatrice
thought it good for him to eat. As to their work, that was

already settled when they married, and it soon became a passion with them. Bernard Shaw, who was their very close friend both at the time of their marriage and afterwards, once wrote from a holiday with them to the lady whom he subsequently married, " I wonder what you would think of our life—our eternal political shop, our mornings of dogged writing, all in our separate rooms ; our ravenous plain meals ; our bicycling ; the Webbs' incorrigible spooning over their industrial and political science."

This last phrase, with its comic turn, almost exactly expresses the Webbs' life and the impression which it makes on the outside world. For there *is* something comic about the Webbs. It is partly because the sight of any two people so perfectly in accord and so perfectly content, in this wicked world, in itself provokes a smile, much as the sight of two lambs playing innocently in a field ; it is also because, having always worked so well together and been so certain that they were right, they have never bothered in the least about what the outside world thought about their mode of life. It is funny to " spoon over social statistics " ; but the Webbs like it. It seemed funny to their friends when, shortly after they were married, they went off to see America and Canada " when they might have seen Greece or Italy "—but they preferred looking at the United States Senate to looking at pictures or ruined temples. Their entire lack of æsthetic sensibility is disconcerting ; so is, sometimes, their determination that time shall not be wasted, as when, for instance, having their own dinners in the minimum of time they stare stonily at the guest who still has food on his plate, or even rise abruptly, leaving him spoon in air. (I have myself once seen Mrs. Webb, in despair at being kept waiting, turn to and eat a banana-skin, the only thing she could find.) In fact, though they are a national monument to whom a memorial should be put up when they die, they have also a faint—a very faint—resemblance to a pair of amiable gargoyles.

They retired from politics a few years ago, after Sidney had served his second term as a Cabinet Minister. During that Government, owing to the peculiar provisions of the British Constitution, he had to take a peerage and became Lord Passfield. He did not want it in the least, being, as a Socialist, opposed to titles ; and Mrs. Webb, equally opposed, and having no reason for changing her name, flatly refused to do so. There was a first-class row ; the Court, the leading Civil Servants, and Society were horrified, but she had her own way, and is still officially to be addressed as Mrs. Sidney Webb. After retiring they made their great journey to Russia, where they were received almost as the father and mother of the Revolution, since it was known that Lenin had spent some of his years in prison translating their *History of Trade Unionism* ; and they settled down to write their Russian book in a house at Passfield in Hampshire which they had bought some years before, having characteristically advertised for one which had " no dogs, no cocks, no children in the neighbourhood." There they live, two people who in a world not too well-adjusted have lived the happiest of lives, have done more for the advancement and understanding of Socialism and the improvement of the people than any one else, and have always given steady and selfless generosity and encouragement to those younger than themselves.

ROSITA FORBES

X

ROSITA FORBES

ROSITA FORBES is the youngest of all the women who have figured in this book. It may be for this reason, or there may be no connection at all ; but, whatever the cause, it is certain that she possesses an element of irresponsibility which is to be found in none of the others. The others, for the most part, took or take life with great seriousness ; they are, as *Punch* used to say in the last century, "intense," and they have or had a purpose in their lives which they set themselves to fulfil, whether or not it was always pleasant. I do not mean that Rosita Forbes is purposeless ; but that she gives the impression of having done the things which she has done mainly because she thought it would be amusing or interesting to do them and not for any more esoteric reason. She enjoys, moreover, most aspects of life ; she has plenty of personality; and there is something about her which the French call *gamine*, and for which the nearest English equivalent is " cheek "—though the meaning is not quite the same. As an illustration, it is said that she once travelled to Russia with a party of earnest inquiring Englishwomen, and rapidly caused it to divide into two opposing portions, of which one thought that she was a dangerous vamp and they would be compromised by being seen in her presence, and the other that she was a dangerous vamp and they had never had such an exciting time in their lives—these opinions being expressed of a woman who took to exploring because she found social life in London, with all its opportunities for "vampishness," so extremely boring!

Furthermore, she has never been afraid of asking; she has never accepted that anything or any person, whether it be a leaky boat, a recalcitrant camel, or an obstinate Government official, should get in the way of anything which she proposed to do, and she fairly soon discovered that if you simply ask for what you want, without considering the many excellent reasons why you should not have it, the odds are that the persons in authority will be so flabbergasted that they will grant it to you almost before they know what they are doing.

Rosita Forbes, among Englishwomen of to-day, has what the economists call a "scarcity value." There is nobody who is in quite the same position. She is not a professional explorer, as a good many people think she is; for, as she herself is the first to explain, the name "explorer," among those who are qualified to judge, means something quite definite. To be a real "explorer" you must either have made a journey into places where nobody sufficiently educated to keep a journal has ever been before—which is not so easy as it once was now that so much of the surface of the globe has been investigated —or, at the very least, you must have travelled in country which has not been adequately surveyed and have made a contribution to the geographical knowledge of it. There are women of other nationalities who follow this profession, such as the Swiss Ella Maillart, and there have been English women explorers such as Gertrude Bell ; but the only occasion on which Rosita Forbes did any exploration in this real sense was on her journey into the Sahara on the trail of Rohlfs, the German, to find the holy places of the Senussi.

She is not, then, properly an explorer. What she can rightly claim to be is the only Englishwoman of the present day who combines a passionate love of travel in the most outlandish places with an ability both to write about them in a way which the British public can understand and appreciate, and to be interested in, and sympathetic with, the problems and troubles of the people among whom she travels. Not that she is not a serious traveller ; the fact that she has received medals both from the French Geographical Society and the Geographical Society of Antwerp is sufficient to prove that. But she is not only a geographer. She is, in fact, several people rolled into one : a traveller first and foremost ; an inquiring mind, second, which wants to understand, and not merely to gape at, the places and peoples among which it travels—her grasp of facts and the shape of the world incidentally has increased enormously since she wrote her first book ; thirdly, a journalist and lecturer who can write and speak either solidly or lightly, as required, with great effectiveness ; and finally, she has written novels as well. And as the number of English-women who travel in strange places is very small indeed, and those who are capable of writing about them vividly on their return almost infinitesimal, Rosita Forbes is in a unique position.

Her early life seems to have left a much less deep impression upon her than in the case of some of her contemporaries. She has written no autobiography ; and her biographer must try to reconstruct it from scattered and casual reminiscences given either in con-versation or in some of her published works.

She was born in Lincolnshire, one of four children of a not-too-wealthy Lincolnshire squire by the name of Torr. Somehow, or otherhow, she was given an education of sorts, some of it at home under a governess, and some of it at school in London—it is all a trifle vague. Children now at school may note, perhaps with envy, that she was good at examinations—which certainly makes school life much easier—and also that she had a gift for picking up languages easily. The second of these qualifications is of obvious value ; unless a would-be traveller can easily learn to chatter (whether correctly or incorrectly does not matter so much) in a language not his own, he will

ROSITA FORBES.

never be a real traveller. He will be a globe-trotter or a Cook's tourist, but he can never hope, if he has not a command of the language, to penetrate any distance into a civilization other than his own. The first may sound less obviously useful ; but there is no doubt that the qualities which make a " successful examinee "—*i.e.* the ability to seize rapidly the important facts about any subject and to remember and reproduce them when required—are exactly those which also make the successful journalist. We may therefore conclude that Rosita Forbes was well equipped from the start for the career which she chose.

Neither examinations nor foreign languages, however, provided her with her keenest interest in early life. According to her own accounts, her first interest, as a child, was to be allowed to hunt all the time—an ambition which was frequently frustrated ; and her second interest was in maps. As she says in the book called *Adventure* (which is the only book in which she has given us any connected autobiographical details), " I always collected maps, and I preferred the kind decorated with stiff little ships, sails bellying in a breeze which looked like a comet, with unicorns or savages to decorate the wilderness. . . . The curly red lines across African deserts had the fascination of a magnet, and I hoped fervently that the pioneers who were writing their names over the blank spaces would leave just one small desert for me." On an expedition to the Sahara she must have realized some of that ambition—although nobody could really call the Sahara a " small desert."

She did not wait long to put her ambitions into effect. She was probably an impatient child ; for, in the book from which I have already quoted, she herself suggests that she suffers both from impatience and from laziness : from laziness because " if we get into camp late and some native happens to make good coffee and there are a few cigarettes left, it is almost more than I can bear to shorten the precious moment of relaxation in sunset, star-rise, or the light of a brush-fire, in order to write up a diary and a route report, to examine blistered human heels and the sore backs of mules, to ration fodder, fuel, and food, to argue over the price of supplies and the shortage in somebody's cartridge belt " ; and from impatience because, more briefly, she cannot resist the temptation to " hurry the East." Most people who have ever travelled at all will sympathize with her in both these moods, even if they have never seen the East, and never been tempted to do more than to hurry a Western railway porter.

However that may be, it seems that her impatience was not a late growth, but began in early life. For at seventeen she married, and married, at any rate partly, in the hope of realizing her early aspirations. She married Ronald Forbes, a soldier bound for the East, hoping that, as his wife, she would be ordered to proceed to all manner of places—China, South America, or Arctic or Antarctic ice-floes—at a moment's notice; rather a story-book idea of the soldier's life, though in the days of the European War it may have been more easy to realize. The marriage did not last very long. It was a good deal later that she married her present husband, Colonel Arthur McGrath. But it came up to expectations in at any rate one respect. She did " go places " ; she saw India and China and Australia ; and when she parted from her husband she went home *via* South Africa, her first real experience of lone travel being when she scandalized the imperial authorities by trying to ride north from Durban across the Zambezi. On this occasion she was frustrated —possibly she had not yet arrived at her full powers of defying authority—and returned to England by a more orthodox route. Back in England, she joined an ambulance that was going to France on war service, and served for some time as an ambulance driver. She earned two medals from the French Government for her war service, though of her driving she says that she alarmed British generals on leave more than any amount of shell-fire !

After some experience in France she came back to London and drove an official car for the British Government. Before long she was looked up by a friend, who had been in hospital and was now released, and who said she was tired of London, and asked Rosita, in a casual way, if she would not come round the world with her. This friend was the companion of her first *wanderyear*, which is described in her first book. She appears there

under the name of Undine, after the water sprite in
Fouqué's book, because, says Rosita, she had moongold
hair and no soul and because she could not keep out of
water. " There was not a river in Fiji, not a stream, a
lake, a bog in Siam or Cambodia that my elusive companion did not fall into. Any one but Undine would
have been drowned twenty times over." She also, it
would seem, possessed the great gift of ignoring all
opposition, and when informed that a journey was
impossible, would merely say, " Oh, yes—when do we
start ? " A good companion with whom to begin a
traveller's life.

Rosita got leave from the Government, and they
started from New York. It is amusing to see, following
their progress in the book *Unconducted Wanderers*, how the
character of the tour changed as they proceeded. As far
as America and Hawaii, it would seem, they were tourists
much like any others, even if the middle of a European
War was rather an unusual time to choose for making their
tour. But as they proceeded westwards they got more
and more unconventional, more and more untidy, until
by the time they reached China they had already become
the kind of traveller who goes in all directions and by all
routes save those which the authorities would prefer, gets
into one scrape after another, and relies on the same
authorities to pull them out.

Their adventures on this tour were chronicled in
Unconducted Wanderers, which according to its author did

not sell well, in spite of a laudatory review in the *Times Literary Supplement*. The publisher thought it was original " because it had such a feminine point of view "—a criticism which must have annoyed Rosita, for she refers to it more than once in later books. She is not in any sense of the word a violent feminist, but she can be made very angry when English journalists, and to a less extent Americans, assume that if a woman has succeeded in doing anything that makes a splash, it must be because she had a man behind her doing the dirty work. All the same, *Unconducted Wanderers* has a " feminine point of view " ; it is a book about two girls touring, and could not possibly have been about two men. It is, also, not nearly as good as some of the later ones. The acuteness of observation, and interest in the real life of the countries she was to visit, which caused people like Lord d'Abernon to write weighty prefaces praising her work, was yet to come.

After the *wanderyear* she went to Paris, trying to pick up work as a journalist at the Peace Conference. For some time she had little success, and merely hung around newspaper offices, living on pretty short commons, and trying to persuade the editors of Paris newspapers that she knew how to write. After a while, however, she fell in with an editor who wanted a series of articles on French colonization in northern Africa, and was lucky enough to make him believe that she could write them. She was sent to Casablanca on the Atlantic coast, taking

Undine with her, and from there gradually drifted across northern Africa, picking up her copy as she went, until they reached Massawa, a thousand miles away on the shores of the Red Sea—Massawa, which since Mussolini's recent adventures is known to more people now than it was then. At Massawa her partnership with Undine came to an end. As she expresses it, Undine wanted to go on " seeing things," whereas she had begun to want to " know things " ; and when she took to studying Arabic seriously instead of being content with a few useful " travellers' phrases," such as " Wash everything everywhere at once," and " It's much too early to stop," they both realized it was time to part.

She herself went through Abyssinia to Khartoum and thence to Cairo, where the British authorities asked her to go on to Damascus and see what information she could pick up about the Emir Feisul's new Arab kingdom. From that commission dates her transformation from a casual traveller into a serious student of politics ; for in and about Damascus in 1920 she first came across Arab Nationalism, and fell in love with it. Having done, as quickly as possible, the job for which she was sent, she turned herself into a journalist and lecturer doing propaganda on behalf of the Arab Nationalists ; and it is rather curious that her single piece of exploration, the expedition to Kufara, was undertaken less for its own sake than in order to equip herself to write with authority. To this day the Arabs, from Morocco to Egypt, from Palestine to

Mecca and Iraq, are her abiding interest, and unfortunately it seems that it may be very long before that interest ceases to be needed, very long before the British and French Governments succeed in clearing up the confusion and distress produced by their own policy during the European War, when in order to induce the Arabs of the Near East to revolt against their Turkish masters, they made them large promises of freedom and territory which when peace came they found themselves unwilling or unable to fulfil. (In the particular case of Palestine, where the British Government managed to make the extraordinary blunder of promising the same country to two peoples, the Arabs and the Jews, the unfortunate results, in riots and ill-feeling, have penetrated to the notice even of the ordinary newspaper reader.)

In the winter of 1920–21 Rosita Forbes started on her expedition to Kufara, in the Sahara, the sacred place of that fanatical Moslem sect of the desert, the Senussi. Kufara had been visited before by the German explorer Rohlfs, but his maps, or many of them, had been stolen from his tent in a hostile Bedouin raid, and the information about the desert route and the oases was considered to be inadequate. She left Benghazi, the capital of Italian Cyrenaica, in November, and arrived back at Alexandria (in Egypt) in February, having visited all the places she set out to see and mapped her route.

The full story of that expedition is told in her first long book, *Secrets of the Sahara*, which was written as a journal while she was actually *en route*. Naturally, it cannot be reproduced here, for the excitement of a travel book lies in its separate incidents, and it would be utterly spoiled if one tried to cut it down. But what the reader of her books notices particularly about it is how far the writer has progressed from the casual globe-trotter who two or three years earlier had set out round the world with Undine. She had spent a long time, she tells us, preparing for this expedition ; and a good deal of the time, in spite of her uncanny gift for languages, must have been spent in an intensive learning of Arabic, for she went into the Sahara disguised as a Bedouin woman, and that not for a casual week-end party, but for a three months' journey in which she would be up against it all the time. She had as protection a letter from the Emir Mohammed Idris es Senussi, the ruler of the country, expressing his willingness to receive her, and a passport from his brother, Sayed Rida, authorizing the Sitt Khadija, a Moslem working for the good of Islam and the Senussi, and A. M. Bey Hassanein, to visit the country. The Sitt Khadija was Mrs. Rosita Forbes ; it is a name and disguise which she has used since on expeditions, not always with the same amount of success.

When she came back to Alexandria she found herself a distinguished person. Government officials were grateful for the information she had brought, and there was a considerable amount of public interest. She was asked to deliver papers, lectures, etc. ; pressmen and photographers scrambled to get interviews ; and on her return to London she was summoned to Buckingham Palace, to tell her story to the late King and Queen. She has set it on record that she was afraid that they would disapprove of the scarlet heels on her shoes, and more afraid, as she sat between them with her map on her knees, and they pulled at it alternately like the Red Queen and the White Queen in *Alice in Wonderland*, that the precious document would come in two. Even if there were some people who sniffed, who talked darkly and irritatingly of " a man in the background," it must have been a pleasant time.

Her next adventure was also in connection with a Moslem chief, the Sherif el Raisuli, called the " Sultan of the Mountains," in Morocco. Her publisher was very anxious to get an autobiography of that enormous man, who from his mountain fastnesses had disturbed the calculations of several European Powers for many years. Rosita Forbes undertook the job, went to Tetuan in a blaze of publicity—which rather tickled the object of her journey than otherwise—and returned, after many long interviews with Raisuli, with a largish book which consists to a great extent of the experiences and philosophy of the Sherif, taken down from his own mouth, and a letter written by him at Tasrut with a pointed wooden stick

and thick black ink, the beginning of whose translation
runs :

'" Glory to God, on Monday the 7th day of Moharram,
the holy, the first month of the year 1342 [in the Moslem
calendar], there came to visit us the beautiful, the precious
pearl, the learned, well-educated Sayeda Rosita Forbes,
the Englishwoman."

After that, and on the strength of it, she visited the
United States professionally, as an author and lecturer,
in the winter of 1924–25. There, she tells us, she received
her first lessons in popular journalism, from an editor
who refused to publish some articles on Palestine because
they were too florid and unintelligible.

" Do you think," he asked, " that Lizzie would understand these ? " And then added, " You know there are
more Lizzies than any one else in the world, and it's her
type of mind you've got to get at." She rewrote the
articles, and, she says, " I never forgot the comment."
Some of us, however, are grateful that she did not remember it to the exclusion of everything else. It may be,
and no doubt is, essential to write newspaper articles with
your eye on Lizzie ; but there are other people than
Lizzies in the world, even if they are not so numerous, and
one could not hope that Lizzie would really enjoy discussions about the clash of Eastern and Western ideals
in Persia and Iraq, for example. As one correspondent

wrote from Manchester, " I do like reading your travel books, but, just when I am all excited over an adventure, I come upon pages of archæology and geography. Please, Mrs. Forbes, do write one book that is all adventure, with no information in it at all " (!). If she had heeded that request, however, she would not be of more interest than any of a dozen popular journalists.

Since 1925 she has performed a great many journeys, and written books about some, though not all of them. Some of her books have been light, some serious, as the journeys have been undertaken with a light or serious purpose ; but they have led her into all manner of different countries and among very different peoples and ways of life. To make only a brief catalogue—which will probably turn out to be incomplete :

She went to Abyssinia to make a travel film, rode through that ancient country before Mussolini had laid hands on it, saw the ancient city of the Queen of Sheba and the underground city of Lalibela, which is all dug out of the red rock, and came back with eleven thousand feet of film which was labelled *From Red Sea to Blue Nile*. She was commissioned by a paper to write an article on Reza Khan, the Dictator of Persia, who began life as a stable-boy, before he became Shah, borrowed the money to get there, and succeeded in finding her subject and writing her article. She sailed a twenty-foot open dhow across the Red Sea in the midst of the winter gales, with a crew of eight Arabs, only one of whom had done the journey before; and from that adventure, with no excuse, she emerged alive. She tried, disguised as a Moslem pilgrim, to complete the holy journey to Mecca, the goal of all good Moslems; but for once her disguise failed her, and she was compelled to return. It may be mentioned here that part of the difficulty of disguising oneself as an Arab woman is due to the fact that unsophisticated Arabs still resemble the patriarchs of the Old Testament and admire what the Bible called " marrow and fatness." In order to be really honoured among them, a woman would need to be so fat that she could hardly walk. Western women, according to present-day fashions, do not run to fat; and Rosita Forbes is actually as thin as a lath. This caused her some difficulty, and deep commiseration from her supposed blood-sisters, when she was trying to pass as an Arab woman. One, more frank than flattering, assured her that she looked like an " undressed snake," and advised her to " cover yourself well. For often a man may be deceived by clothes." To any one, however, who has seen Rosita Forbes in the flesh, the idea that she could pad herself out with extra covering into a woman who would attract Solomon is ridiculous.

These were probably minor journeyings. She aimed, however, at considerably more serious game at times. About 1930 she went on a journey to the new countries of the Near East, some of which, such as Syria, Transjordania, and Iraq, did not exist before the war, and all of which are being profoundly changed by the impact of Western ideas and Western invention upon their ancient customs. She started from Angora, the capital of that new Turkey which Kemal Ataturk is trying as fast as possible to turn into a modern State; she went through Syria, Palestine, to the borders of Iraq, and all over the huge realm of Persia, where Reza Khan is making the same effort as Kemal; and she published her observations in one of the best and most serious of her books, *Conflict*, in which she notes such contrasts as those between the new towns in the Persian oilfields, which are like a town in middle-western America, and the ancient bandit-haunted villages of Luristan. It is a tribute to her open-mindedness, as an observer, that in Palestine, in spite of her passionate love for the Arabs, she was able to appreciate and admire the exciting experiments being made by the Jewish colonists.

Not long afterwards, changing her scene of operations, she went to South America, and in another book, called *Eight Republics in Search of a Future*, she wrote about life as she had seen it in Brazil, the Argentine, Peru, Bolivia, Paraguay, Uruguay, Ecuador, and Chile—names of countries which to most young readers are names and nothing more. Many even of their elders are not really aware, for example, that Brazil is bigger in area than the whole of the United States. In this book she attempted, as well as describing the countries, to tell her readers what their politics were and what their future was likely to be. She does not, naturally, know the South American nearly as well as she knows the Arab ; and events have moved so rapidly that her prophecies are now out of date : nevertheless, it is still interesting to read.

She went to northern Russia—Leningrad and Moscow —as I have said, with a party of earnest inquirers into Soviet education, and subsequently she entered the same country from its south-eastern corner, coming up northwards from Afghanistan to the Caspian Sea and the Volga, and so getting quite a different impression of that vast area which is the U.S.S.R. At the time of writing she is considering making an expedition from Kenya Colony on the east coast of Africa to Nigeria on the Gold Coast on the west. When that is done there will be little of the world left that she has not had a look at except the polar regions ; and no doubt she will go to the North or South Pole if she feels any inclination.

This is a bare summary. It simply states where, and in regions how far apart, Rosita Forbes has travelled. To do more, to try and describe what she has seen on her travels, would take a great deal of space, and could be no more than a re-hash of some of her own books— and would not be interesting ; for, as I said before, the excitement of travel books lies in the separate incidents, the black magic and mass-hypnotism of the East, the eating of *kat* (a drug made of small juicy leaves) in a harem in Arabia, propriety among an Indian caravanner's wives, who might be stripped naked without harm, but would be killed if they showed any scrap of their faces, propriety in an American hotel, which wakes visitors at four in the morning to tell them to lock their doors, etc. etc. Those who want to know more about them must read her own books, where they will find, as well as the more solid work, plenty of " travellers' tales," credible and incredible, ordinary and tall, of the kind which travellers have always told since the great Greek Herodotus first set the fashion.

THE END